The Breakthrough

A Spiritual Journey that Led to One Woman's Independence

ZAHRA HEYDARI

BALBOA
PRESS

A DIVISION OF HAY HOUSE

Copyright © 2012 Zahra Heydari

All rights reserved. No part of this book may be used or reproduced by any means, graphic, electronic, or mechanical, including photocopying, recording, taping or by any information storage retrieval system without the written permission of the publisher except in the case of brief quotations embodied in critical articles and reviews.

Balboa Press books may be ordered through booksellers or by contacting:

Balboa Press
A Division of Hay House
1663 Liberty Drive
Bloomington, IN 47403
www.balboapress.com
1-(877) 407-4847

ISBN: 978-1-4525-5968-1 (sc)
ISBN: 978-1-4525-6126-4 (hc)
ISBN: 978-1-4525-5967-4 (e)

Library of Congress Control Number: 2012918645

Because of the dynamic nature of the Internet, any web addresses or links contained in this book may have changed since publication and may no longer be valid. The views expressed in this work are solely those of the author and do not necessarily reflect the views of the publisher, and the publisher hereby disclaims any responsibility for them.

The author of this book does not dispense medical advice or prescribe the use of any technique as a form of treatment for physical, emotional, or medical problems without the advice of a physician, either directly or indirectly. The intent of the author is only to offer information of a general nature to help you in your quest for emotional and spiritual well-being. In the event you use any of the information in this book for yourself, which is your constitutional right, the author and the publisher assume no responsibility for your actions.

Any people depicted in stock imagery provided by Thinkstock are models, and such images are being used for illustrative purposes only.
Certain stock imagery © Thinkstock.

Printed in the United States of America

Balboa Press rev. date: 11/20/2012

To God for talking to me when nobody was around
To my dad for teaching me how to love
To my mom for teaching me how to sacrifice
To my daughter for believing in me
To my son for inspiring me
To Dr. Wayne Dyer for giving me confidence
To my teacher Oprah Winfrey for telling me
"Education gives you wings to fly"
To my dog Lucky and his big loving heart.

Forward
By: Daniel Hamidi

In December of 2009, my mother, sister, and I visited our family in Iran. We went to see my great-uncle's family in Tehran one night for a gathering. My relatives were delighted that the three of us were there visiting them and the general mood was positive. It was the first time that they saw my mother in her full freedom. She was a dove that suffered for copious years in a cage, but finally got to extend its wings and fly. I remember looking into my relatives' eyes and seeing their astonishment; they were almost stupefied by my mother's pure, unfettered joy.

I also remember thinking as we had dinner that night about the fact that my sister and I were not the only ones who endured so much agony with my mother. While we were the combat troops in the war against a fervent, daunting force, my relatives were the folks back home who prayed for us and anxiously awaited news of our survival or death. They might have been on the opposite side of the globe when all the hardship happened, but they were always there for us in spirit, and for that I would like to thank them.

As dinner started to end, I heard something that I would never forget. My great-uncle loved music; he used to be a singer himself. He played a popular Iranian song called "Hamechee Aroome" by Hamid Talebzadeh. Though I usually am not a fan of Iranian pop music, I absolutely fell in love with this song. I was in awe over how relevant the lyrics were to my own life. The part of the song I loved the most was:

> All is calm
> I feel so elated
> You are by my side
> I pride myself
> You have given your heart to me
> This is obvious from your eyes
> I'm so well off
> All is calm

This song demonstrated what I felt towards my mother and her genuine, unconditional love for me. She was always there for me in the toughest of times. I am absolutely proud to say that I have the most outstanding mother in the world. She always has been there as a shoulder to cry on when I am feeling melancholy. My mother is always willing to do absolutely anything for me. She is my inspiration as I walk through life. Without her valiance, I would still be in the miserable state I was in when I was younger. Without her unrestricted love, I would not have the strength or encouragement to go through life as I have been. Without her compassion and the way she understands me, I would not be able to express any emotion at all. My mom is the bravest, kindest, and most amazing person I know.

I hope that all of you who are planning to read my mother's journey through life get the encouragement, the power, and the motivation to change your life for the better. Do not sit back and let something you know is wrong continue to happen. Do not watch your life and the lives of those around you decay without making an effort to improve those situations. As Gandhi so famously stated, "Be the change you want to see in the world."

As you read this book, think of what a transformation my mom went through. Think of how much courage she must have had to go from being an obedient and passive nineteen year-old bride to a self-providing forty-five year- old single mother. And ultimately, think about how much it took for her to reveal all of this to the world to inspire others to walk through the independence road. As motivational speaker Scott Backovich said, "Change what you hate with what you love." My mother hates seeing people suffer, and she loves helping them. She has used this passion for inspiring people to get past their problems as a marriage and family therapist. Hopefully, this book will have the same effect. I applaud her for this magnificent feat, and I hope you take it and let it change the way you see the world.

The Breakthrough

One phone call changed my life the way that I had never dreamed was possible. I was visiting my uncle and his family in Tehran, Iran with my mother, my older sister who was fifteen at the time, and my brother who was eight. This trip was similar to the previous visits with lots of delicious food, loud conversations, multiple hugs, and a deep sense of love in the room.

It was almost midnight and we had just finished dinner. I was cleaning up the kitchen with my sister and two cousins. My mother and aunt were talking (make that gossiping). My uncle was telling jokes to his son and my brother. However, my father was not there. He was sent by his work for some special training to Tabriz, a city about a 5-hour drive from the city we were living in, Ghazvin. As you could imagine everyone was doing just fine. In the midst of all this joyfulness, the phone rang. This phone call taught me just how fragile life really is and how everything could completely change, with good memories fading away being replaced with ongoing depressing tragic moments.

When my uncle picked up the phone, his tone of voice changed rapidly. This is a man who prays 5 times daily, talks to God all the time, and praises God continually for everything he has in his life. He is a very peaceful calm man, but this phone call made him go crazy. I remember because this was the first time that I witnessed him cry and scream at the same time. I heard him say, "Yes, he is my brother!" After that he was crying.

He fell down to the ground, started to hit himself and asked, "God why? Why my brother? Why not me?" He kept saying this for few minutes and then his wife and my mother kept asking him what happened until he finally answered. He told us that the police called to let him know that his brother, MY FATHER, had been in a very bad car accident that day and he is in the emergency room in a very small city close to Tabriz. They were going to transfer him early in the morning to the Ghazvin hospital. My mother kept screaming and asking God to keep my father safe until tomorrow. My teenaged sister and my teenaged cousins were sobbing as well. My brother was quiet and I was crying, knowing this was very bad. I did pray that the body they found and took to the hospital was someone else's body. I prayed that it was just a simple human mistake. I prayed that my father was sleeping at peace in his bed in his room in Tabriz. I believed my prayers, and I was at peace. I stopped crying, and tried to help everyone else.

That was a long night; nobody was able to sleep. We all just wanted to drive to where he was, but because my uncle talked to the police and was told that my father was in the ambulance being driven to the Ghazvin hospital, we decided to get ready and try to get to the hospital as soon as possible. During this whole time my peaceful, religious uncle was crying loudly and had a hard time containing himself, let alone anyone else. He called my other two uncles, and in about half an hour they arrived with their families. No one was able to sleep. Crying and praying were the only two things that seemed feasible at the time.

I will never forget the car ride from Tehran to Ghazvin. I was the only one who was sitting very quietly and kept thinking everything is going to be fine since the policeman who called made a big mistake. The man in the ER was not my father; he was someone else.

When we finally got to Ghazvin my uncle, who was driving the car, took us to our home instead of going directly to the hospital. He told us the police said my father will be arriving at the hospital shortly. As soon as we got home, one of our neighbors came to my mom and told her how sorry she was about my father's sudden DEATH. My father was dead. My mother kept hitting herself, and cussing at God and my uncle. My uncle kept saying I am so sorry, the neighbor is right. According to the police phone call last night, my father died a few minutes after the accident and never made it to the hospital. Oh, my God! This was so bad! Life was absolutely terrible for a long time; blissfulness seemed like a strange concept.

The funeral was an enormous event. My father was a very kind, loving, and compassionate man. He didn't have any enemies, but had too many friends. In order for you to imagine his funeral, all I can say is that everyone in the city of Ghazvin was sharing the same pain that my immediate family was experiencing. My mother kept passing out and could not handle all this. She had to go to the emergency room and was put on a very strong antidepressant right away. This was the beginning of a new chapter in her life called depression. My mom has dealt with this for over 30 years now.

A Story of True Love in Iran

Mehry (my mother) was the last child to be born before her father decided to get married for the 2nd time. Mehry's father was a very well-known army general who also owned a few villages. Her mother was a very kind, loving human being who liked the comfortable life her husband had created for her. She was a social, warm homemaker whom anybody would love to have as a mother. Mehry's mother believed that a girl does not need any education because her husband will work to support her.

Predictably, Mehry stopped schooling when she finished 5th grade against her will. Her mother kept telling her that she needed to learn to cook, clean, and be a good housewife. This was very difficult for Mehry, since some of her friends continued to go to school. It started to get more difficult when Mehry was about 14 years old. It's very common in Iran, when a girl is in her teenage years, that the possibility of husbands would come along. The way this was done is the parents of the eligible young man would start searching or investigating to see who would be a good beautiful wife for him. If they found someone that could be a possibility, the parents or the family members of the young man would ask the girl's parents if they could come for an afternoon tea. Having said this, since Mehry was from a very well-known father, and she was tall and attractive, every week the family had lots of afternoon tea gatherings or as Iranian people would call it "khastgari." Since she was the only daughter her parents had, they kind of spoiled her and did not force her to get married right away.

When she was 17 years old a very handsome young man whose name was Ali came with his family for the khastagari, or afternoon tea. Mehry was speechless after seeing how good looking this guy was, and of course for Ali, it was the love at the first sight. After he and his family left Mehry's house, he told his parents that no matter what it takes, he wanted Mehry to be the mother of his children and to live happily ever after with her. His parents were not so sure since Ali's father was just a farmer and did not have any money. They were worried about how Mehry's father would agree to such a marriage.

His parents were right. The next day they got the message that since Ali is not from a rich family, and did not have any higher education, he could never marry Mehry. This news was such a tragedy to Ali and Mehry. She cried for 3 days and after that she decided she would wait for Ali to come back when he has more to offer to her father.

Guess what? Ali did what he had to do. He got his AA degree and joined the army which was a very respectful job in Iran. He was the first in his family to finish high school. In the meantime, do not ask me how, but they dated secretly. We are talking about very traditional religious families with strict rules. I call this the power of pure love and faith.

When they got married, it was a match made in heaven from day one. Ali was a very kind, caring, humble, hardworking, religious man. To make him even better, he was very tall, had beautiful hazel eyes, and loved God. Ali's job as an army officer required for the family to be moving every few years, which worked out well with Mehry's easy going personality.

They started having kids one year after they got married. Adding the chapter of parenthood was easy in their marriage since they both had very similar values. Although they came from very different family backgrounds, raising a family in a warm, loving environment was very important to both of them.

Four years after my sister's birth, I was born. I was told a few different stories about my first experiences on planet Earth. My mother wanted a son very badly. After the birth of my sister my mother was not happy that she had a girl, but she accepted it since she knew her next child would be a boy for sure. Well, here I come. I was born in the middle of my grandmother's living room and not in the hospital, with the help of an experienced midwife who had no schooling. She got her talent by just practicing and it actually worked. By the time she delivered me she had already delivered over 54 babies who all lived.

When my mother first saw me and heard the news it was a GIRL, she started to cry and cuss at the world. My father on the other hand, came to the room, and started to make my mother feel guilty about her nagging. He told her, "God has blessed us with this healthy, beautiful baby, and you are complaining? Just look at those eyes and be grateful." It took my mother a few days to accept the bad news about not having a son, but she did her best from day one to take care of me. The good news for her came after my brother was born. She finally had a healthy, strong boy. He was full of joy, but my mom did not mind spoiling him at all. He got everything he wanted.

Being the Middle Child

As a middle child, I learned how to become invisible at a very young age. I had a demanding older sister who wanted to have everything in the world since I could remember. Even now she is a collector and loves fashion. Since she was very young she had her own voice when it came to dressing herself, decorating the house, cooking, and anything that is fun and artistic. God has blessed her with unlimited talents, but being artistic is very costly.

Going back to our childhood, she knew exactly how to dress to impress, and my father had a limited income but loved to take care of his kids' needs. My mother was a stay-at-home mom, who enjoyed cooking and entertaining. So every new year it was a dilemma for my mom to buy my sister new outfits and new gifts.

My sister would make my parents drive her to Tehran, the fashion capital of the world in Iran. We lived in a very small city which was about a 2 hour drive to Tehran. It was very common for my family to spend 2 to 3 weekends every month in Tehran, since all my parents' families lived there at the time. My mother never complained about this drive; she actually liked to talk to my dad in the car. But anytime this trip was because of my sister's shopping, my mom was not happy. You could easily see and feel the resentment in her mood. She just could not hide it.

With my sister's expensive unique taste, it was a very important mission for her to look for hours and try to find the latest shoes, clothing, or perfumes. Then when she was back in our little city all her friends were impressed. Though my mother hated shopping with her, she had to do it because my sister was too young to do it on her own. My mother used to gets angry with her because if my sister liked something, she did not care about the price. My mom kept reminding her that our dad had very limited income, but my sister just did not get it. I remember when I was 10 years old sitting and pretending that I was sleeping. My mother was venting to my father about my sister's expensive tastes, and he told her to never say no to our children. He told my mother to use the savings if necessary to buy whatever we all needed.

My brother had his own moments as the spoiled baby of the family, plus he was a BOY! My mom finally got her boy. He was such a perfect, handsome baby boy who brought so much joy to the family. He was unpredictable and full of energy. What I love about him is that he has been able to keep up his fun loving personality. He could walk into a room full of strangers, and after few minutes he could talk to everybody and they would all like him. He is very charismatic. So having said all these you all could imagine how my parents felt about having him. He got everything he ever wanted! If there was a little delay on his demands he would scream and cry so loud that all the neighbors would hear him. In order to prevent the public shame, my parents gave him almost everything he wanted.

I remember how we all took a family trip and went to Mashhad, which is a very nice religious city. My brother was about 5 years old. He wanted every single car that he saw, or he would scream. My parents kept buying him almost everything he asked for, but in the middle of the day everyone was getting tired of his show. My parents were frustrated about how he needed to have everything. So when he asked for another toy my parents told him they could not buy any more toys for him. He started to scream so loud that people came out of their stores and started screaming at my parents. It was so embarrassing! He did not give up crying for a long time and yes, he got his car. I wish my parents had bought the car before his show. Now you have a snapshot of what my siblings were like when I was growing up.

I learned since I was four years old that my parents loved me, but they just had too much to handle with the other two. I decided to give them a break. I never asked for special toys or fashionable clothing. I was a happy child who had compassion for her parents. I used to feel sorry for my parents and angry at my siblings for bothering them so much. I was worried about how my parents would pay for all the ongoing demands from my sister and brother. I don't write this to make anyone feel sorry for me because all this helped me to become a very strong flexible person.

The Gray Days

One night when I was 10, I woke up in the middle of the night because my parents were arguing loudly. My mother was talking to my father about arranging my sister's marriage. My sister was only 14 years old at the time, and one of my parents' friend who had a 25 years old son had called my mother and asked her about the possibility of having my sister marry their son.

After my mom told my dad about this idea, he said, "She is only 14, and thus it is too soon to talk to her about this. She will have time to get married in the future. She needs to finish school, go to a good college, and become financially independent. I will not allow for my daughter to get married at such a young age. Just call our friends and tell them that I do not like the idea. Blame everything on me. Do not bother telling our daughter about this because she is way too young to hear this." My mother countered, "This young man is highly educated and is from a good family. We could agree with his parents that the two would get engaged for a while and then they could get married when she is ready. We can't lose this good opportunity." She convinced my father to talk to my sister.

The next day I saw my sister and father talking peacefully. After that, my father talked to my mother; there was nothing peaceful about that conversation. My mother was infuriated, and passionately yelled, "This young man would make her happy. Why does she need to go to college or get a job? She eventually will need to be a good mother and wife anyways."

Anyways, my mother arranged for the young man came with his family to ask for my sister's hand for marriage a couple weeks later. My father told my sister that day, "Do not worry; I will take care of this." After they left, my sister told my mother she is not going to get married before she finishes not only her high school, but also her college education. I heard my mother crying, saying that my sister does not need an education. According to my mother, she just needed a good husband like my father.

My parents had different ideas of raising children. One was pro-education, and believed in financial stability before marriage. The other believed that a good, solid husband is the answer to all life's problems. My mother knew my father's love for her was immense, and she believed my 14-year old sister needed a good marriage as well.

After the proposal, my father promised my sister that he will not let anybody, or anything disturb her path to education and independence. My sister tried to take school more seriously, and she became an honor-roll student.

After my father's sudden death, everything started to seem to die in the lives of my sister, brother, and mother. My mother's personality changed – she became a shadow of her old self. Depression became her new best friend, and it stole my mother's smile. I absolutely loathed depression because my mother had clearly lost the battle to it. She wore black for more than a year and stopped bothering to color her hair (my mother started to have gray hair since she was in her late 20s, and she always colored her gray hair brown, but after my father's death she just did not care).

My sister was an emotional and sensitive fifteen year old that had her own ways of dealing with the death of our father. She would go to her room, close the door, and listen to the most depressing Iranian music. Her room remained locked for hours. I remember a few times when she told my mother she was too sick to go to school. When I would come back home she would be in her room, isolating herself. My mother was especially worried about her after my sister stopped talking to us. She was angry, and lost her passion for school, even though she used to be an extremely gifted student. She was very intelligent and managed to receive spectacular grades even though they were not of the utmost importance to her. My father definitely had been pro-education, and he had big dreams for all of us. I remember one time when my father and sister were talking about what she would study in college, and how my father always kept telling her that she would get into any university she would like to because of her intellect. My mother, on the other hand, was not into education and never really talked to my sister about college.

My talented sister started to try to learn cooking new recipes. For some reason she got interested in decorating around this age too. Now that I look back I think God talked to her, and helped her to heal, by planting all these creative seeds in her beautiful soul.

As much as my brother and I loved her cooking, we were worried that her passion for school was fading away. Even a year after my father's death, she was still depressed and kept herself busy buy trying new recipes, decorating, and of course crying few hours a day.

My fun, energetic baby brother started to get quieter and less joyful. The worst part for him was the nightmares he got when he went to sleep. His nightmares continued for almost five years. Almost 2 to 3 times a week, my brother would cry loudly in his sleep, call for my father, and then would scream and call for my mother. He kept telling our mother, "I forgot his voice. I forgot his laugh. Tell him I am sorry for being so spoiled and crying for toys. All I want is to remember his voice. I want to die if I can't remember him. I need to remember how he used to play with me." This was just so sad. We all felt so sorry for my sweet baby brother. My mother used to wake him up, wipe his tears, kiss him, hold him, and talk to him until he would go back to sleep. To be honest, my two siblings and my mother were handling my father's death so badly that I was worried about losing one of them.

Sometimes to cope with my father's death, I would day dream that everything around me was just a movie. This wasn't my real life. My father would be home today around 5:00. My mom is busy cooking her amazing dinner for all of us. My sister is busy looking at the latest fashion magazines, trying to figure out what she has to wear tomorrow to look pretty. I am just getting ready to go to the park on my bike with my friends.

While I was at peace in my head with these great images, I would hear my mother crying loudly. Sometimes just looking at her eyes gave me a reality check. HE WAS DEAD. OUR LIFE WAS DEFINED BY SADNESS. Then while sitting in a quiet corner with my school books on my lab, pretending that I was studying, I started to feel peace by pulling my thick curly hair out of my scalp. I would do it for a while, until all the pages in the book in front of me were covered with thick, black hair. Then I would get up and take all the hair to the trash can, and would close my book.

Nobody noticed anything about my hair loss until almost one year after. One of my mom's friends asked my mother why my hair was getting thinner. My mom noticed this and started to cry. She kept telling me, "You are going bald! How could you do this to me! Now I have to deal with this too." I felt sorry for my mother, and stopped doing it for a while, but still did it from time to time. My mother decided to take me to get a short hair cut when I was 14 years old to prevent this from happening. I stopped playing with my hair for a while, and it started to grow. I never became bald but I lost a lot of hair. I am now 45 years old, and I still play with my hair when I get anxious, but I do not pull it out of my scalp anymore.

So overall everything in our household after my father's death was just GRAY. My family started to feel some warmth and love when my three loving paternal uncles and their families came to visit us every weekend. They tried so hard to bring some joy to our broken hearts while they tried very hard to cover their own sadness in front of us. We all would go to my father's grave every Friday. My youngest uncle is blessed with a gift to make people laugh with his stories. God bless his big heart, he tried even harder than usual to make us forget about our pain with his funny jokes, but we still felt hurt.

When I was 12, almost one year after my father's death, my sister got introduced to a young successful business man through my mother's friend. He was amazed with my sister's beauty, and sense of style. My mother was getting worried about how my sister was isolating herself in her room for hours, crying, and not showing any interest in school. She was not failing but she just was not in to it at all anymore. My mother decided a good marriage could solve everything since it did in her own case. She talked to my sister for hours every day, and finally convinced her (without forcing her) that the businessman was too good to be true and she should just go for him.

My sister was seventeen by now and got married to this man. He lived in Tehran, and after they got married they started their lives as a couple in Tehran. My mother decided we should move to Tehran to be close to my sister as soon as she heard my sister was pregnant.

So I started getting used to living in a big city. It was not easy for me, but my brother eventually grew to like it. He made a lot of friends right away, and he was never home. With the blessing of God, I too made amazing friends that would remain my friends to this day. I kept hiding the deep secret about my father's death, because I did not want anybody to feel sorry for me. It was easy to feel like everybody else.

I remember my first day of school in Tehran. The teacher asked everybody to say their names and what their father did for a living. I started to feel anxious; I just was not ready for this. Why would I have to talk about my father who is dead? When it was my turn, I said my name and I said my father is a retired army officer. It felt real. From that day, I never invited anybody to our house. I just did not want anybody to know how bad my life was, and I did not want anybody to feel sorry for me.

My sister had her first boy when she was 18. Her marriage was BAD, very BAD. Every time she had a fight with her husband, he would bruise her in some areas. She told me everything. She wanted to divorce him when she was only a few weeks pregnant, and he did not agree (in Iran, it was very hard for a couple to get a divorce without the husband's consent). It was sad to see her beautiful eyes so sad all the time.

He gave her a new affluent life style; he was rich and successful. She liked the luxury and tried to just make the best out of her life. She loved her husband to some degree, and she loved her family. She knew she couldn't get divorced unless he agreed, so she just lost herself in him. My sister got pregnant again when she was 19. As a teenager she became my role model.

My mother was so depressed and weak from my father's death that my sister had tried to hide a lot of the hardship she suffered from her. Sometimes, her bruises were just too big to hide though. Every time she got hurt by him, I thought about THAT PHONE CALL. I knew if my father were alive my sister wouldn't be in this marriage. She would be a hard working nineteen year-old student enrolled at a great college. She would be in a much better place. My mom eventually realized she made a big mistake by forcing my sister to get married, but it was too late. My sister's self esteem was gone, and her soul was bleeding every day. I started to feel angry and resentful towards my mother, and I began to pray that God would protect my sister.

These were my teenage years. I made sure to be available to my sister any time she needed any help. I loved her two boys more than my life. She was busy all the time, preparing her home for big dinner parties that her husband hosted. Because he was such a successful, well known business man, my brother-in-law had two to five dinner parties in his home with his clients and business partners a week. She was an amazing cook, loving hostess, and a very gifted decorator. My mother and I helped her take care of her sweet boys with love. My mom and I felt sorry for my sister and did our best to alleviate her pain.

School was fun with my friends. After our move to Tehran, I lost my desire to do great in school. My mother was too busy with her depression, my sister became lost in her daily crises, and my brother was occupied with a constant desire to be out of the house with his friends. So this was how everything was. Nobody really expected for me to do great; I just needed it to get by and I did. My life from age 11 to 19 was filled with lots of gray days.

The Sudden Move

Day dreaming about their wedding day is normal for little girls. I believed in true love and still know love is one of the most magical things in life. I was 19 years old and tried to get in to a university. In Iran, at the time I finished high school in 1985, getting accepted to a university was extremely hard. You had to be very gifted or have lost a father or brother in the war between Iran and Iraq. In my case I had neither of these. No family member died from the war, thank God, and I was not the smartest girl in my school. So right after finishing high school, I felt lost. I knew I did not want to get married, since I was able to see my beautiful sister's daily pain of ongoing physical and emotional abuse. My mother was worried that I may get too old or get raped, so she was hoping and trying to arrange for my marriage.

At 19 years old I had never had a boyfriend, but I had my ongoing daydreams about what real love is and I kept praying to my dear God to bless me with a kind, loving man when I was older. I was not sure how old, but I knew it was not 19 years old.

To make the story short, I met a family at the home of one of my mother's friends. This family took some pictures of me, explaining to me they thought I was pretty and they just wanted to have my picture. I agreed as agreeing became a part of me. I lost myself in the process of agreeing with everybody. The family showed the picture of me to their son. I met him and the next day it was very clear to me that I did not want to marry him or be part of his family. There was nothing wrong with them; I just did not feel good about marrying him. I told my mother and she fainted.

After she recovered she called my aunt and uncle, whom I love and respect dearly. She asked them to be witness to what she had to say. This is what she said. "If you do not marry him, I will never forgive you. I will not come to your wedding if you marry any other man." Her main point was he seems calm, peaceful, and she cannot handle another bad, abusive marriage for me since my sister, who was married at 17 through an arranged marriage, was in pain. She added that if anything happened to her after today it would be my fault since I was causing her severe stress.

Wow! This was very powerful and sad at the same time. I loved my mom and did not want to lose her or make her sick. I lost my father when I was 11and she was the only parent I had left. Of course I did what she wanted me to do. I married a man that I met three weeks earlier and had gone out with him four times to do some shopping for the wedding. He was 10 years older than me. He seemed peaceful. He was educated outside of Iran.

After we got married we went to Europe for our honey moon. I was happy to travel, so we left one week after we got married. The honey moon was over before it started. First of all, I never really felt loved by him at our wedding day. He would not hold my hand or smile deeply. He seemed miles away from me and everyone else at our wedding day. I was surprised and shared my concerns with my sister. She said not to worry as he is very shy. So now we are on our honeymoon and I still felt very disconnected. While we were in Europe he told me he doesn't have a lot of money, but he has enough to take care of me. He brought me to USA one week later. We started our married life. I cried any time I talked to my family back home. I missed the busy streets, the bakery by my house, and how my mother always made sure we had fresh cookies for our afternoon tea. I felt worried and guilty about not being there for my handsome loving teenage brother who was only 15 years old and was recovering from the death of our father slowly. Now he had to go through another loss of his teenage sister and best friend. We used to listen to music together every day after school. Music made us forget about our pains for a little while. We also liked to make fun of our depressed mother, and how we hated eating her boring food, but at the same time we both felt very sorry for her. It was painful to see how she was getting older and sadder every day. I felt extremely worried for my sister and her two beautiful boys. I missed them like crazy. I felt hopeless and out of control about my marriage and in the process I lost myself.

Around this time I started to fall in love with my husband. I had never been kissed or touched by anyone. He was older and controlling, just like a father. Since I lost my father eight years before, he became all that my lost, low self-esteem wanted. I did not know English; he was educated and was very fluent in English. I tried to get used to the idea of being far from my love ones. I did my best to push myself to blend into his family, and make them become my family too. I was desperate to be loved and connected to his family. They were very kind, to me, and did their best to make me believe they really liked me. He started to take charge of everything and I liked it. I started to accept my life in America.

The Birth of My Sweet Angel

Less than a year passed before I became pregnant. I had the most amazing gift from God when my beautiful daughter was born. Looking at her eyes for the first time I felt paralyzed. I was in labor for 36 hours, and finally the doctor realized I should have a C-section since the baby's health was in danger. So becoming a mother was not an easy thing for me, but she came and she brought an ongoing, ever-lasting joy to my life from that cold winter day the minute she was born. I felt so proud to be her mom and I wanted to make sure she would have a better life than my mother and me. I was not homesick anymore. I was too busy being in love with my miracle of life, that I did not take any bad thing in my life seriously, including our financial problems and my husband's controlling behaviors.

When my baby girl was two weeks old we took her for her first physical exam. It was one of the worst days of my life. The doctor stated my daughter had a heart murmur which is common among new born babies. Usually something like that would heal on its own before the age of two, but in some bad cases a child with that could die at 15 and never be in any sport or have any children. This was so bad! I couldn't stand up and I felt weak. I cried all the way home, and kept asking God why my baby.

My daughter ended up having open-heart surgery when she was nearly three years old. It was one of the most difficult things I had to go through when I was 23 years old. God was there and He took care of her. Much to everyone's surprise, she ended up running cross-country and track while she was in high school. Anytime she finished a race, I cried and thanked God for protecting her. Anytime she got awards for being the fastest runner among many teenagers her age, I whispered to God thank you.

My daughter has the most beautiful eyes. Her eyes could tell stories about her beautiful heart that was not healthy and normal. Her eyes could tell how strong and confident she has been since she came into this world, and unfortunately her entrance to her parents' marriage that was far from normal and loving. From the first day she came to our home from the hospital, she brought pride, joy, and courage to my heart. She planted the seed of courage in my heart. It took a long time for my courage to grow, but it did. Unfortunately she had to witness how weakness could break you into pieces at a very young age. She has seen her mother cry a lot of times over and over about so many things. I know God gave me this angel so I would stay alive. It sounds irrational, but it is true. She kept me grounded. I never tried any drugs which would have been easy for me to do. But knowing she loved me and was waiting to see me with those big beautiful eyes, I would look forward to seeing her. I loved being a mother! Looking back, the severe pain I would endure made me appreciate having my daughter 100 times more. Every time we talk I always make sure I tell her I love her and how proud I am to be her mom.

Going for a Career

I came to the USA when I was 19 years old, and had my daughter when I was 20 years old. We had bills to pay, and ongoing arguments about money. I felt guilty about not working. I was taking English classes in the local community college and added some reading and math classes too. It was very hard to learn anything while there was so much financial stress at home. I decided to learn skills that could earn money quickly. I went to beauty school and completed my training in 9 months by going full time. I hated taking my daughter to the day care early in the morning and picking her up at 5 in the evening. She only cried once. She was so mature, accepting, and strong. When I dropped her off the first time, she looked in my eyes when I told her I have to go to school, but I would be back soon and take her to the park. I love those eyes! Her big beautiful eyes were filled with tears. She cried and held on to me. I learned from those tears that she loved me and needed me to be strong. I made a promise to myself to do my best to never see those tears. I learned being a mom reveals one of the most powerful strengths in the world and that is love. I talked to God while I was driving away from the day care. I cried and asked God to help me never put my children before any other human being. I asked God to help my baby understand that I had to go to school because we needed money for our very basic needs. I also got tired of listening to my daughter's father nagging about money. I learned to talk to God on daily basis, asking Him to take away the guilt I was feeling for not providing a stable strong family life for my beautiful child.

The bad memories from beauty school outweighed the good memories. It was so hard be away from my baby for 8 hours a day. I had to use my timecard every day to check in and check out. If I was late for few minutes they would mark me absent. I finished the training in 9 months. I knew I was not a naturally talented and gifted hairdresser, but one of my teachers, Mr. Sparton, told me I would be very good as a hair dresser for two reasons: 1) I am easy to talk to and can carry on a conversation with anyone at any time and I actually care about what I hear. 2) I am beautiful and people like to interact with beautiful people. So based on those reasons he said I would be able to be a good hairdresser.

I became friends with someone I met at the beauty school. We bonded since we were both young mothers, had no best friends, and had ongoing interpersonal conflict with our husbands. My problems were worse than hers, so we started to talk share our problems and became very close.

I was 21 years old, married for two years, felt no love from my husband, felt trapped, felt isolated, and was homesick. Around this time I finished beauty school and got a job as an assistant hair dresser. I worked five days a week for 10 to 12 hours a day. It was such a hard learning experience. I had to wash hair, serve coffee, and be very friendly and social. On top of all that I had to look very stylish which was part of the job requirement.

My Hair Dressing Days

I did hair for 10 years from 1990 to 2000. I loved the fashion part of it. Getting ready to go to work every day was like going to a fancy party. I started to make friends with fun, carefree, and very talented people. This was a very fancy beauty salon. When I was a student, a client came to me just to style her hair and she told me about this fancy beauty salon which was very hard to get in and was expensive. She stated she went there only twice a year (for Christmas and the Fourth of July) since it cost so much. She believed I belonged to that fancy place because of my style.

I went there two days after I got my cosmetology license. I just got dressed up and went to the interview. Wow! The place was magnificent! I wanted to be a lucky client and get my hair done there! The music was loud, everybody was dressed to impress, everyone was trying so hard, running around, and all the clients looked like hair models. I felt at home. I was "in love." Yes it was a love at first sight experience. I told the three owners the truth; that this was the first place I was trying to get a job, I was a mom, and I was married. To make matters even more interesting, my English was not good at all. Still, they loved me! I got hired right then and was introduced to all the staff of about 45 people that same day. I was told I was gorgeous; they loved my accent, my natural curly hair, and admired my sense of style--thanks to my lovely sister who sent me her old outfits from Iran. What I loved about this place was that it was very dreamy to me. It had models showing off the fashion of the local designer woman's clothing store. The three owners were from three different parts of the world, and I blended very well with the various cultures. The only big change was they told me I should change my Iranian name to something easy and American. I agreed because I was young and in love with the place. I had a goal and I wanted to do anything I could to become a hair dresser with my own assistant. I liked the idea that I would be helping my husband with the bills too.

The two years that I assisted were very hard, but rewarding. I wanted to learn all the skills from the best of the best in the field, and as you remember I was not a naturally gifted and talented hair dresser. So it was not easy shampooing hair, talking, looking very stylish, and trying to learn the tricks to mix hair colors that would look like natural hair. I tried very hard not to cry at home in front of my husband. I kept all the sad feelings inside. I had days that I felt like a slave, no lunch or any breaks for 12 hours, had color stains on my outfit, smelled like perm solution, and my hands were burning from the bleach damage. I kept telling to myself that THIS SHALL PASS. I kept thinking about the end result, and when my super sensitive boss, would talk down to me I did not keep quiet. I defended myself and he was speechless. He told me he had no idea I could get defensive too. The worst part was I started to feel very guilty about not being around my beautiful daughter. I knew we were financially struggling and I wanted to help my husband, although I was getting paid minimum wage. It was a lot of hours and tips helped too. My mother in low was very kind to me and my daughter. She tried to baby sit when my husband was busy, and I had to work. I will never forget her help, and I am always grateful to her.

After two years of assisting and a very clear argument with my boss, I got my own station and became a hairdresser. I loved the idea of creating great hair, and started to build my cliental. I became busy in a short time, based on three reasons: God, my way of talking and communicating with all my clients (making them feel they matter to me,) and the last reason was my willingness to become better every day.

Although I was doing very well at work, at home things were not right. My husband started to show me he was in charge of all my basic daily decisions. He started calling me a loser, an uneducated hairdresser. He kept referring me as a pretty face with a small brain. According to him my brain was the size of an almond. He started to verbally abuse me on daily basis. The worst part was I believed him. I loved going to work and leaving him behind. I was busier at work and got my own assistant one year after I got my own station. So my goal was accomplished. I was a busy hair stylist in this fancy place with my own assistant. I was making a lot of money, and my husband was happy about the money, but that was it. He wanted more children and I didn't for two reasons: I didn't love him enough to have a child with him, and I didn't want to take another big responsibility. I felt guilty that I was not able to spend enough time with my daughter and did not want to do the same thing to another child. I tried very hard to be the best hair dresser I could and be the best mom. I was not sure what to do with my husband. I had very low self-esteem about myself. I was worried that I could never make it without him. He kept calling me a stupid shampoo girl and how he was ashamed to tell any of his friends or co-workers that his wife was just a loser hair dresser. Just to clarify something, he was just in sales, nothing really fancy, but he had the audacity to make me feel useless and bad about myself.

I loved making my own money, creating, interacting with my clients, but the best part was when they were sharing with me their life stories. I felt so special when they would feel connected to me. All my clients became like my family. When I was a brand new hair dresser with only two weeks hands-on hair dressing, I had the opportunity to do this walk-in client named Karen. I loved her British accent. She was in her 40's and seemed very kind and easy to talk to. I was worried about how I was going to do with her hair, before I met her, but she brought peace and confidence with just being herself. We talked about what she wanted to do with her hair. She simply told me she trusted me, and I could do anything I felt was good for her hair, just not to cut it too short. Wow! I was speechless. I felt very creative, took my time, and did the best I could do with her hair, and it turned out amazing. The best part was we connected on a very deep level. She became my best friend, my mentor, and my spiritual mother. She was like one of my guardian angels. God talked to me through her in different times in my life. From the very first time we met, she talked to me about going back to school and doing something more meaningful. I felt guilty sometimes when I would make so much money, while being with my clients felt just felt like being with my loved ones. While my career was booming, my self-esteem stayed very low. My husband kept calling me bad names at home. Part of our daily routine at home was ongoing verbal abuse, occasional physical abuse, and sexual abuse.

The Abuse Begins

The first time my husband hit me I felt very disgusted and small. I was hoping my daughter wouldn't remember it. The very first time she was only five weeks old and we were invited to one of my mother's friend's wedding party. I was only 20 years old and felt stressed out to get my baby and myself ready. I packed the diaper bag, got my baby ready, and finally got myself ready. We went and my husband brought his cousin who was not invited to the party. He and his cousin kept drinking. I was all by myself with my baby. She was not happy since it was loud in there, and I was tired by 11:00pm. We got there at 7:00, so I just wanted to go home. During the four hours we were there my husband did not hold the baby once. He was just talking and drinking with his cousin. I felt lonely, sad, isolated, sleepy, and just wanted to be home. He agreed to leave at 1:00 am. For five hours I had the baby all by myself. She was crying, I was tired, and he finally agreed to leave since the party was over. We came home. I cried while I changed. I was feeling sorry for myself and my baby. He raped me for the first time. He said he had to have sex so he could sleep, and he did not care if I was too tired. I just cried and closed my eyes.

The next day I realized I left my hand bag at the wedding which had my wallet in it. I told him and he got so mad he slapped me and called me an airhead. He kept screaming at me for hours. All I said was sorry, you are right. I was happy my baby was too young to see how hopeless her mother was.

From that day I developed this fear of my husband. I knew if I misbehaved I would pay for it. So going back to hair dressing my work was a safe escape from him and my marriage. I developed two different personalities. One was passive aggressive and obedient at home. The other one was happy, social, outgoing, friendly, fun, and a strongly motivated hair dresser at work. Around my daughter I was the strong happy carefree, fun, energetic mom when he was not around. My husband kept asking for more children while I was thinking about divorce. When my daughter was six years old I had tried hard to fix my marriage. We even saw a therapist. My husband promised he would change and I hoped for that miracle. Since I came from a broken home where my father died when I was just a kid, I wanted to give my daughter everything that I did not have. A warm, loving home was the first thing she needed it. Or maybe these were just my own excuses for not having the self-esteem, inner power, and the family support to go for divorce. The combination of all these made my marriage worse every day. My husband was becoming more aggressive and I was losing myself more and more every day.

I believed I was just a stupid, uneducated low-life mother and wife. When my daughter kept asking for a baby sister or brother I felt maybe a baby would change my husband and make this marriage stronger. I wanted to become educated, always have my home clean, invite my in-laws over all the time, cook, clean, and be all that my husband wanted me to be.

I started to take one class at a time at 7:00 AM twice a week for four months at the local junior college and liked it. I was told by my husband I must study biology, became a dentist, or pharmacist. The last career advice was to go get my real estate license and work for him. I tried all that just to please my husband and none of them worked. I failed my real estate exam twice, and I barely got a passing C in my biology class. I hated all the science stuff. My accounting class was a disaster. I was earning an F, but the instructor dropped me after two weeks knowing that I could never pass his class and the F would be bad for my records. Things were bad at home, and I started losing my interest at work. All his words were in my head and I felt very lost.

The Birth of My Brilliant Son

When my daughter was six years old I agreed to have another child, since my daughter kept talking about wanting to have siblings, and my husband wanted to have a son. He kept talking about the baby every day. We tried for one year and finally I got pregnant. Unfortunately, I miscarried after two months. This was so hard. I cried for days, and my husband told me it was my fault and blamed me for days. I felt like a failure, believed him that I was a loser, and it was my fault I lost the baby. I went to Iran for a few weeks after to relax, and I felt sick and tired. My sister took me to her doctor. He did the pregnancy test and told me I was pregnant. I got so happy I hugged the doctor and told him my baby boy is here. He was very surprised and asked me why I was so sure. I told him I just knew. With my daughter I also knew that she was a girl.

The pregnancy news was great and it felt very right. I was very grateful and happy. I hoped for a stronger family bond and unity with my husband. My daughter was so happy about the baby boy. I started talking to him and reading books to him while I was pregnant. I read in one of my books that classical music is good for pregnant mothers and their babies, so I did that. My energy was good and I loved working throughout the pregnancy. I felt great about myself and had so much hope and faith that everything in my marriage would get just better and it did for a while.

The birth of my beautiful son was long and painful. He looked happy, content, and I loved his curiosity. He was born at 7:18 pm after 27 hours of labor. He did not sleep until 11:00 pm. All the nurses were surprised about how he wanted to take everything in. I thanked God for this healthy baby boy, and I cried, because I wished my father was in the hospital so he could hold him. I realized I was madly in love with this little man, and I prayed God would help me to provide, promote, and protect this angel.

My husband was happy about the boy he got, but he did not know how to show his love and appreciation for his family. The more I got into being a mom, the more he started to drift away. He started to go hunting with a guy who was 10 years younger than he was and had a history of domestic violence. He had gone to jail for beating his wife. This new hobby had good and bad outcomes. The bad one was he started to take off from work as often as he felt like. There was no boundary. He did what he felt like doing. Since he had his own business it was all up to him and he took advantage of this. Also he started to become best friends with someone that was more carefree than him. They started acting like single people with no families. The good part about him going hunting was I loved being away from him. It felt so free and it made me very strong. I had to be a single mom from August until mid-February. Any time he felt like going hunting he would.

The love of for my sweet, energetic, smart, and loving little boy kept me very active and happy. I had special date days with him, and we loved going to Disneyland together. Holding my hands he kept telling me how happy he was and that was the most soothing music to my ears. My son was eager to learn from the time he was only 15 months old. He started to ask me about planets, religion, and world history when he was only four years old. I loved his curious mind! Of course I had no answers, so he would make me take him to a book store and get him the resources he need. I loved how he kept me busy and distracted from all the negative energy in my marriage.

Being involved with my two great kids was my antidepressant. I loved doing what they wanted. My hair dressing job was another way for me to forget about the ongoing verbal and occasional physical abuse.

My Journal Entries

Now I will share some of my personal journal writing. Oprah talked about journaling and how she likes it, so I got back to it and it felt good to get things off my chest. This is a snap shot of my life.

11/09/98

24 minutes on the treadmill, 10 minutes of toning; my goal is to have a flatter stomach. No dinner after 5:00 pm. I feel happy to be healthy, being able to enjoy the day from the beginning to the end. I like wearing something pretty, putting make-up on my face, and feeling like a beautiful woman. I'm happy to go out to have breakfast with my sweet baby boy. I enjoy having a cup of coffee in front of him, and the best part was not cleaning up the table after we finished. It feels so good to be served even in a cheap coffee shop. After our breakfast we went to Newport Beach and I was able to discover a very nice area in Balboa Island. We walked for about 25 minutes then we went to Mother's Market. I loved the whole day, had a great day, and I am thankful for everything.

You can see I was able to have my husband and my problems out of my head and my sight, daily workout even for 20 to 30 minutes, and spend time with my baby boy one-on-one. It was just perfect.

This was the time of my life that I was working three days a week, 8 to 12 hours day as a hair dresser, had my own assistant, had a strong clientele, and was making $ 3500 to $5000 a month for only working part-time, which was great. Since my husband kept talking about education, this was the time I was going to school twice a week just one class at a time. I was a room mom at my son's preschool once a week. I loved looking at the way his eyes would sparkle anytime he would notice me in his classroom. With my daughter she felt very secure about the way we connected together, so I never felt she may get jealous of the time I was spending with my son. I was worried about the ongoing verbal abuse in our home.

11/26/1998

I have been very depressed for the past few days. Starting Friday his mood started to change since he was cleaning and we had guests for dinner. I did all the grocery shopping and cooked this Korean meal that I just had learned from my best friend. He did not stop calling me names and was cussing while he was cleaning. I just ignored him and cooked. Cooking is very healing for me. Overall the dinner party was great. We had to go to an Iranian restaurant for his friend's anniversary. So we did and we had a good time.

The next day, Sunday night, we had to go to a house party. It was very crowded with a house full of people. My baby boy got overwhelmed as he was used to going to sleep early. He was very fussy around his bedtime (a typical Iranian dinner party starts after 8:00 PM and goes at least until midnight). So my baby was sleepy, and he was used to going to bed around 7 to 8 pm. I asked my husband nicely if he could give me the car keys so I could take the baby for a car ride, hoping he would fall sleep in the car. He ignored me. (All the men were talking together and all the woman were gathered in the kitchen talking.) So I approached him while he was around other men. I asked him very politely and he ignored me one more time. This time I touched his ears and said to him just give me the keys. I need to drive the baby around so he could sleep. He gave me the keys, and I left with the baby.

The Breakthrough

While I was driving around with the baby I was listening to Madonna and crying and feeling so small, stupid, and hopeless. I felt like I was in jail and there was no way out. I was just so mad at him for ignoring me and at the same time controlling me. So after the baby fell asleep, I came back to the stupid party. For the last 2 to 3 years I did not enjoy going to all these gatherings for so many reasons. They were very long (at least 3 to 5 hours), they were loud, and there were so many people talking. There's lots of gossiping among the women too. I felt very disconnected but forced myself to go to be a good wife and a good mother.

After I came back with the baby sleeping in my arms I took him upstairs without any help, came down, and just tried to fit in as best as I could. My husband finally agreed to leave around 1:00 AM but did not offer to help with the baby. So I went upstairs and carried the baby to the car. My daughter, who was 10 years old, sat next to the baby in the back seat. My husband had more than few drinks, but stated he is not drunk and wanted to drive. I did not like the idea but agreed. I was too depressed, and sleepy to argue. He started to drive, and in about 5 to 10 minutes he pulled the car to the quiet small alley and stopped the car. I asked him where we were and why he did not go home. He got out of the car, came to my door, opened the door, and started beating me up in front of my 10 year old daughter who was awake. She started to cry. Thank God the baby was sleeping. He did not stop beating me. I was in shock, and he kept saying to me," Don't you ever try to control me in front of other people. You are a fucking nobody." All I kept saying was I am so sorry. Please stop, our daughter is awake, and the baby will wake up, please stop. My daughter was crying loudly now, saying daddy, please do not hurt her, please stop. He finally stopped and closed my door, sat down, put his seat belt on, and started to drive while he was cussing at me.

We got home, he got out first. I got my frightened baby girl out first, held her hand, took her to her room, hugged her, kissed her, and kept saying I was so sorry to her for what just happened and promised her everything will be OK. She was shaking, crying, and saying mommy I love you, and did it hurt when he was beating you up. I lied and said not at all. He is angry and everything will be fine. He is just angry. I do not know why. So I helped her change, go to her bed, kissed her, held her, and by now 10-15 minutes had passed. I remembered my baby boy was still in his car seat in the car which was in the garage. I told my daughter I have to go get the baby. She got up and followed me. She said she was too afraid to be by herself and wanted to come with me to get the baby. She came down, was holding my hand, and I saw she was crying very quietly. I hugged her again, wiped tears from her beautiful face, and told her not to worry because everything would be fine. I wish I was right. I knew I was telling her big fat lies. So we got to the garage, got the baby who was two years old and almost 40 pounds out of the car. I carried him to his room and put him down on his bed. My daughter was holding unto my skirt this whole time, since I couldn't hold her tiny hands while I had the baby in my arms. After I put the baby down in his bed, I took my daughter back to her room, hugged her again, put her in her bed, and told her she needs to sleep, that everything will be fine. She said she was worried he may hurt me again. I said do not worry. She kept talking about what had just happened one hour ago, and how her father could do that. I just held her, kissed her, told her a story, and helped her to focus her attention on something else, or at least I hoped I did.

All this time he was sitting downstairs watching TV, which was very normal. Since the baby was born almost 2 years before, he has slept downstairs in the sofa while he is watching TV. As I was hoping this is just what he would do tonight, he came upstairs to the bedroom, took his belt out of his pants, and told me he is not finished with me. He started to beat me up again, this time with his belt, and it was not going to stop anytime soon. I asked him why he was angry, told him I was sorry, please stop, you will wake up the children. He did not listen. I started to cry, begging him to stop. I was feeling the pain in my face, my arms, and my legs. I was thinking about my father. If he was alive, would I be married to this jerk today? Would I be this hopeless? I was thinking about my mother and her huge mistake by forcing me marry this jerk, just because I was beautiful and she was trying to get rid of me before I got raped. I wanted her to see me get raped. Anytime he wants to he rapes me, and this is a man she thought would protect me. I thought about my poor sister, and how she had to deal with this physical abuse on a daily basis with her abusive husband. I thought about the people I know at work, at my children's schools, at my own school, my friends, and what this image right now with my husband beating me up with his belt in our own bedroom for no clear reason would make them think. At last I thought about the phone call that changed my whole life when my father died and my self-esteem died with him.

Learning to Cover the Pain

That night I had bruises all over my body, I had pain in my head, and I just could not stop crying. After he was done beating me he went downstairs and started to watch TV. My kids were sleeping. I was shaking in the bed. Part of me was fearless and wanted to call the police to have him arrested right at this moment so he would be out of my life and my sight and my heart forever. Part of me was afraid to make any move. I was worried that he may get angry by my movement and would start beating me up again. So I just sat in the bed and kept crying quietly, shaking and cussing at myself for being so weak, for not having any family around me, and for not having the backbone to call the police.

The next day I noticed my arms and legs were in pain and were also bruised. I was going to go to the doctor since I started to shake again, but he did not let me go. He started being very nice to me and wanted to take care of me. I looked at him and wanted to vomit at him and at myself. I just wanted to cry and started to pray. I asked God to help me get out of this mess. I begged God to show me a way, to escape from this man. I cried and prayed to have enough power to do what I have to do. I heard a voice telling me hang in there, your day will come. Just hang in there, take care of those kids, and take care of yourself. You and your kids need each other. So I did.

12/31/1998
THURSDAY 9:10 PM

There are a few more hours left in 1998. I am praying 1999 will be a better year for me and my kids. I am praying to be a stronger, more confident person. I am seeking to become a free woman who is God's best friend. I do not want to walk next to my husband at a party. I hate everything about him. God, I do not know how long these feelings will last. I hope it is not temporary. I hope I will stay strong. I hope he would let me go easy, because I really want to go. I want a divorce. God please help me to make the right choice. I am begging you God for a better year in 1999.

Well I did not end my marriage. I was just in survival mood. He told me during a few daily arguments that if I want a divorce I could get one. But he would kick me out of the five-bedroom home. He would take away my kids and the two cars. He also used to say he would pay for a one-way ticket for me to go to Iran, become a whore and support myself. The worst part was I believed he had the power to do all that. The only thing I was sure of is that I would never become a whore. So it was very hard to be in a same home and share two amazing kids with a man that I was not in love with and had no way to get out.

Around this time he kept calling me names in front of our kids. His favorite one was "Dumb-dumb". One day he told me he is tired of taking care of the kids while I was at my hair dressing job, and I needed to stop spinning my wheels and do something productive with my life. He asked me to go to school and become a pharmacist or attorney. I was also feeling guilty being gone three long days, and he was always telling me I was a lazy hair dresser anyway and did not make a lot of money. With all these negative things about my marriage and I was losing my passion for work, I started to think about school.

One day one of my clients came. After I put her conditioner on I put her under the hair dryer. She started to read her book which was called Couples in Crisis. I loved the name of the book and asked her why she was reading that book. She told me she was getting her master's degree in marriage and family therapy, and this was one of her classes. Oh my dear God! You just talked to me. I got so fired up that I was up all night thinking how cool it would be to learn about dealing with couple in crisis.

That same day my friend and mentor Karen came to get her hair done. She was working on her degree, and she was almost 20 years older than me. She encouraged me to go to school, get educated, and start growing. I believed these all were signs from God. I hoped to learn all the information about people and their problems, and apply them in my own life. I talked to my best friend at work about my ongoing problems at home and she told me maybe I should try to be a more hands-on wife. She encouraged the idea that if my husband is pushing me to get educated, maybe he also needs more of my attention. So I prayed and asked God to help me, to show me a way to make me happier and bring more control in my life. Also I was getting tired of all the nonsense that he was ashamed to tell people his wife was just a shampoo girl. I will share some personal journal entry around that time in my life.

10/10/2000

I am very thankful to God for my health, my beautiful children, and my warm house today. God, please be my best friend. Be my light in the darkness. I need you to be very close to me. I need you to make me more confident. I need you to shine through my house, and my marriage. I need you to go to my husband's heart. Make him love me more and be more what I dream about. Make me enjoy and appreciate what I have in my life today. My goals are to be a better person over all. I want to be able to finish school. I want to have a degree. Please open up my husband's heart to you. I want to be a good role model for my daughter. I need to be an educated person. I did well on my psychology paper and my test. Thank you for being my best friend.

Around this time my best friend at work Emily kept talking to me about God and the power of his love. Sometimes we would pray together at work. We bonded deeply when we both got pregnant at almost the same time. It was my second pregnancy and her first. We both were blessed with our boys who are a few months apart. Today our teenage sons are still close friends. She started to pray for me and I liked talking to her about my problems. This was the time my husband started going away with his friend for hiking and hunting. I was struggling with myself. Part of me wanted to be all that he wanted me to be: obedient, educated, very clean, organized, skinny, and social. I wanted to please him. My friend Emily kept talking about what kind of a woman God wants us to be for our husbands and I listened. I tried to be and do anything that would make my marriage better. The other part of me was completely done with him, had lost hope, and was ready to put him out of my life and my children's lives. I was ashamed to be around him and was disgusted with myself for being his wife. Going back to the phone call when I lost my father, I also lost my self-esteem and did not want my kids to grow up without a father. I wanted to give them what I did not have: a normal family.

11/6/2000

I am very busy at work, home, and school. I want to be 125 pounds for the holidays. Right now I am 133 ponds. I am walking 5 to 6 times a week and watching what I eat helps. My English class is not going well. I need to really practice hard for the next 5 weeks. My husband is the same. I have good and bad days with him. I try to not to think about him. I just block him out of my mind; otherwise I get so depressed that I cannot function.

Today I had lunch with Jody. She is very fun, and I hope we become close friends, even after I stop doing her hair, if my husband would let me keep her. I have been feeling friendless recently. Four of my close friends do not come to our home anymore. I think they all hate my husband and think of me as a weak, ignorant woman. I am trying to love, respect, and please my husband in any possible ways that I can. He has been hunting for the last 3 months any time he feels like it with the friend that I do not respect and trust. My friend Emily has been talking to me about giving love to my husband that is unconditional, and the more I would give, God would help me to receive what I deserve to get.

I am very sure that I will stop doing hair next month. December 22 is going to be my last day. My husband keeps telling me he will support me if I go to school. I want to concentrate my time and energy with him, the kids, and my school. I am afraid. I tell everyone I am ready, but I just hope my husband will be nice to me.

With all the unsure feelings, my friend Karen kept talking to me about all the benefits of education, and how I was too young to be uneducated. I left hair dressing for good and decided to help myself to grow. Things were just OK at home. I loved being home with my kids when they were home. For some reason, in the deepest part of my heart, I needed to get ready for some hard work at school. I craved stability. Talking to God constantly was helpful. I kept praying He would show me the way to be more understanding, make my husband love me, respect me, and not hurt me.

4/5/2001

It is my birthday. I am turning 34 years old. I am very busy at home and at school. I take the kids to school then go to college four days a week. I am taking economics, accounting, business law, and psychology. I hate all of them except my psychology class. My husband is fine. He is still spending time with the friend that I do not trust, but I am asking God to guide me and show me ways to make my family stronger. We have not been sleeping in the same bed for the last few months which is fine with me. I am happy. My kids are very happy to see me every day and they gave me great birthday cards. I love my good friends too.

I wish my family was here. My sister is getting a divorce after 17 years. She is tired of all the nonsense in her life. I hope she can actually get the divorce. Well, my mother is against her divorce. She still likes my brother-in-law like her own son. I am happy and worried for my sister. She has never worked and doesn't have her high school diploma since she got married at 17. I do not know how she is going to support herself and her two amazing teenage sons. He will do his best to stop the divorce, but my sister is tired of the ongoing physical abuse and his addiction to have affairs. I wish I could be there for her and I wish I had the money to help her. I am mad at my mother for arranging my sister's wedding when she was only 17 years old. I know my sister was depressed when my father died, and although she was an A student in her high school, my mother thought marrying her young would save her from depression. I know I should not be writing about all this on the day of my birthday, but they all called me to wish me a great day, and talked to me about what was going on. Well, enough of all these negative things. I feel blessed to have my two kids. They love me and I love being their mom. I feel good about my age, and I feel good about going to school.

Nothing really big happened over the next two to three years, or if it did I was very ignorant about it. I just tried every day to get closer to God, talking to Him and begging Him to help me stay at school and pass my classes and be the best I could be with my two amazing kids.

While I was learning new things in school about the world and myself, I was feeling more disconnected from my husband. I started to go to fewer parties and enjoyed studying or reading books at home.

My mom came for a visit and she was very disappointed with the way I did not go to all the Iranian gatherings with my husband. She started talking about me to my husband and telling him I needed to change. I didn't really care. I was very focused on three things in my life: my relationship with God, my kids' well-being, and my school. I started to feel resentful toward my mother and how she liked speaking badly about me to my husband. I started to blame her secretly for my arranged marriage that she still denies.

I kept close contact with Karen who was my cheerleader throughout all my schooling. She was very positive, and encouraging. She helped me with some of my essays, and whenever I felt lonely I could call her. My other friend Emily kept encouraging me to get closer to God, and I knew I could call her anytime I needed it in order to feel understood.

The best parts of these years were being able to be in all my kids' activities. My daughter was in high school, and she had cross country and track meets all the time. I felt very blessed to be there for all her races. I loved being a room mom for my son and was in the classroom a few times a week. The highlight of my days were looking at my kids' eyes and seeing how they would light up anytime they would see me. I loved, loved, being a mom! Overall I felt happy and tried to stay positive, ignoring all the negative energy from my husband.

I got my BA in Psychology in the spring of 2002. I felt very proud. It was one of the happiest days of my life. My mother came for my graduation. I missed my father in my graduation. Though his body was not with me, he was in my heart all day long. I was the first in my family to go to college and get a degree. My husband was happy that day too. I thanked God and my friend Karen for encouraging me to go to school.

I applied for the Master's Degree in Marriage and Family Therapy. That year and I did not get in because my GPA was very low. Karen helped me to write my purpose statement for the master's degree program. They wanted students who have a strong desire to help people in pain and also students who had gone through some personal dilemmas. I was sure about convincing them with my dilemmas. I just had a hard time getting all of them in one small essay. Karen took a few days and helped me to do the best I could.

After I got denied my husband was very mad at me. He kept calling me an idiot, loser, and useless. He came home one day very angry and told me I have three choices: 1) have another baby before I get too old, 2) find a job as soon as possible, or 3) start law school or a master's degree as soon as possible. He said he is not going to keep supporting a lazy, hopeless, loser wife, who lounges around the house and watches Oprah every day. I loved watching Oprah every day that was true.

Seeing her face was like visiting my family. I loved listening to her talking about everyday problems. Once she said education is the key to have wings and fly. I never forgot that.

So in my house it was the war zone again. I tried to find a job, but I couldn't. I did not want to have another baby for few reasons. In order to have a baby you need to have sex, and that was not happening in my home. I knew I was not in love with my husband, and did not want to grow old with him. I had a boy and a girl, loved them to death, and wanted to do my best for them. So the only option was trying to start school as soon as possible.

I tried three times to get into the master's degree program. I got denied twice. Before they rejected me a third time, I made an appointment with the Dean of Admissions. I told him I just needed 5 minutes of his time. He gave it to me. God helped me to have a voice. I told him I know my GPA is bad, but because of my own personal dilemmas I know what pain is. I told him about the phone call, my father's sudden death when I was 11, my mother's ongoing depression, my country's war when I was a teen--all the bombing of my beautiful country, my arranged marriage at 19, my daughter's open heart surgery before she was three years old, and my own self esteem issues. I talked only for 5 minutes (I know that is hard to believe). I told him I know what pain is and want to help myself and all my clients deal with pain. I told him please give me a chance to achieve my dreams and do not let my low GPA make me stop here. I thanked him for his time. He called me the next morning and told me he loved the fire in my eyes and in my voice. He told me I was in. I was going to start the three year program in August of 2004.

9/15/2004

I started my master's degree program on 8/23/04. I love the classes.

I went to Iran this summer with my son for four weeks. My family paid for our tickets. My daughter couldn't come because of her cross country practice. It was bad at home. My husband hid my passport and my son's passport for few weeks. He kept saying his work is slow, so we shouldn't be thinking about going anywhere. My family offered to pay for all the expenses. He was in such a bad mood for about two months—all of May and June. I felt very depressed and weak about not being able to do anything about his strange behaviors.

For some reason he started to resent me. I knew it was real and I wasn't imagining it. I woke up July first and prayed God would kill me. I knew I do not have the money, family support, physical and emotional strength to get a divorce from him, so I just asked God to take my life.

After a huge argument he slapped me, kicked me, and left to go to the beach with his cousin. I called my friend Janie, who lives close to me. I asked her if she had time for coffee. Oh my God! I cried and cried the moment I saw her. I told her how he is hiding my passports and is not letting me and my son to go back home to visit my family. I told her about the name callings, and how he is getting very angry every day for no special reason. She was speechless. She told me she cannot believe how I could go on with my life with all these bad things happening. I hugged her and thanked her for listening. I came home, and just prayed. It was very soothing. I looked at my children's eyes, and realized they need me and I am not finished raising them. I apologized to God for wanting to die and begged Him to keep me strong until they were all grown up.

That same day my husband came and told me he talked to my family and told them he cannot pay for our tickets. They told him they had already sent some money for our tickets. So my son and I went to Iran and it was just perfect. My family tried very hard to make me relax, and did their best to show my curious son all the great places in Iran. It felt great, but I was worried about my daughter and kept hoping her father was not mean to her. For some reason I was feeling guilty for not protecting her from him. While I was gone for four weeks my husband called my son and me only three times. My family was very surprised. My mother was feeling guilty about all this. My sister told me maybe he is having an affair, and my brother just hugged me and told me he was sorry about all this. They asked me if I was going to get a divorce and I said no.

Just to make all this just a little more exciting, I had only $15 in my wallet when I left to go to Iran. My husband did not give me any spending money. He said he did not have any, but he called me three weeks after I was in Iran, consulting with me about purchasing a $3 million beach house in Newport Beach. I could not believe it. When I asked him how we are going to pay for it, he told me he will sell our home and get a loan for the rest. I will work full time to help him to pay for the monthly mortgage. When I told him I will be starting school next month and do not think I could work, go to school, and be a mom, he told me fuck you and hung up on me.

I did not talk to him until I got back. I was not sure if he would pick me up from airport. He did. He was in a good mood for about two hours. Then everything changed and he has been in a very bad mood till now. It is so hard being around him. He keeps calling me loser, lazy, and really bad names. He talks to me like that In front of my children. I get very sad, feel small, and want to die so I won't see the sad eyes in my children's faces.

After I came back my daughter told me he and his best friend (the hunting buddy) had stopped talking since the 3rd week of July and my husband had not gone to his home office since then. He had stopped working. I did not take this seriously. Oh, was I wrong or what?! Yes, the best friend ended his friendship with my husband. I never found out why, but he told me it was over.

He started to watch hours of TV. He did not take a shower for days. He was extremely sensitive and he was in a depressed and irritable mood all the time. I was walking on eggshells when he was around, which was all of the time unless he was went hunting. I was so worried all the time about not making him angrier, that I did not even have the time to be fully present with my children and my friends.

The only place I am able to block him out is at school. I love being there. I know I just started and it has not even been a month yet, but I love it. Today he is not home. He is gone hunting and before he left he told me I have to find a job before he is back, which I'm hopeful is at least three more days. He is gone from Thursday through Sundays almost every week. I love it.

He told me yesterday to get out of his life for good. I have no idea what is happening to him. I wish I could afford to get out, but I know I cannot. Last week he checked my grocery store receipt then yelled and cussed at me for wasting a lot of money at the grocery store. I just looked at him and felt so small and hopeless.

I decided I have to get a job. I thought about going back to hair dressing since that is a job I know very well and I could have my own hours since I want to go to school and be with my kids. So a few days ago I got dressed up and tried to look my best. I wore my nice black suit, pulled my hair back, and started to drive around the beach areas. I found this really fancy beauty salon on Pacific Coast Highway with a sign that said talented stylist needed. I went inside and felt pretty and confident. I asked for the manager. He was sitting in the front and he welcomed me. After just 5 minutes he asked his wife to come and meet me. He said one of the stylists had a baby and is not planning to come back. He hired me right there, and told me I could start any day, any time. He loved my accent, my style, and the fact I had 10 years of experience doing hair. I came home, felt great, and thanked God for how he had blessed me today.

On my way home I called my husband and told him I got a job at this fancy beauty salon at the beach. He laughed and said are you crazy or what? That is too far, and how are you going to manage picking up the kids when I am hunting or busy. He called me stupid and airhead. I cried and felt stupid. Maybe he was right. I started to cry and realized how that phone called changed my life. I am 37 years old and still act like a hopeless fatherless child.

7/20/2005

This year was bad. The more I got involved with my school and my kids, the angrier he got. He was not working at all, but everyday talked about how lazy I was and then told my daughter she needs to work too. My mother came for a few weeks. It was so bad what she had to see. I did look for jobs, but with just a psychology degree there are not too many jobs, especially since I have no work experience in that field and I am 37 years old. Money is very tight. Every single day we are arguing about it. I am so busy with homework, grocery shopping, cooking, cleaning, and being a loving mom. It is getting harder and harder.

My baby girl graduated from high school. She asked for a small graduation party. It was just pure hell. My poor mother was here to see her granddaughter's graduation. After what she had seen in my home I am sure she regretted her decision. The day of her graduation party, my poor mother and I started to cook, clean, and prepare for the dinner party. He got up and the first thing he said was to call everybody and cancel the party. I just kept praying quietly, just begging God for strength. I prayed he would get a call from a client or friend so he would just leave the house. Thank God he did. He left and I cried hard. I told my mother I hated my husband and I would never forgive her for arranging my marriage to this jerk. She cried, said she was sorry to me, and kept cooking for the dinner party. With the blessing of God the party was just perfect. My daughter looked happy, and for few hours we forgot about the monster in the house.

Here is another snapshot of this year. My beautiful daughter was going to her prom, just like any normal teenager. My husband did not like the idea of bunch of teenagers dancing together. He believed that is how she will become pregnant. For her prom, he was in a very bad mood. He woke up started to cuss at me for not making him coffee on time. So I made him coffee and also prepared his breakfast. He started talking on the phone, went to the backyard to smoke, then came inside after 5 to 10 minutes. By now his omelet was not hot and his bread was not crispy. He got very mad and told me I was good for nothing. He threw away the breakfast I made and made something else. He was mad and did not stop complaining. He told me today I have to clean the stove, bathrooms, and windows. He took the car keys. I wanted to say I am sorry but not today. Please give me the keys. My baby is planning to get her hair done and go to prom, but I was too anxious to say anything. I looked at my daughter, and tried to talk to her with my eyes. I was just hoping he would go soon and never come back. I was standing a few inches away from him washing the dishes, and praying God would take him far, take his life away today, and make this breakfast his last meal on this planet.

Finally he left almost 3 hours later. My daughter's dance was starting in 2 hours. As soon as he left my daughter started crying and it was loud. I held her, kissed her beautiful face, and told her everything will be fine. At the same time I started to pray, talking to God and begging him to help us to get her ready. Although I was a hair dresser for 10 years, since I stopped doing it for the last 5 years, I did not want to do my daughters' hair or make-up. I forgot how to do it, and I wanted her to be pampered like all of her friends. So I made an appointment for her to get her hair done by my best friend Emily. Well, since I had no car keys to take her I cancelled the hair appointment. Now I decided to do the hair and make-up myself. Well, I had no hair spray. I couldn't think clearly, so I just begged God for clarity and directions. After just few minutes, I realized I could ride my bike to the local beauty supply store and get the hair spray she needed. I did it. I got the hair spray and came home. I talked to God and prayed for creativity and strength. I tried to hold my tears back while I was curling her hair. My heart was breaking because this day should have been a great day for her and why didn't she have a normal peaceful life? Why am I doing this to her and to myself? How come I am so weak? She felt my sad feelings and started to cry. I hated myself at that moment. Her tears were like a knife cutting my heart and soul to small pieces. I started to cry with her, held her tight, told her I was so sorry for all her pain, and kept curling her hair. She looked amazing. My husband's sister drove her to her high school. I told her we cannot take a chance to have her date pick her up from our house. So this was just one small view into our stressful lives with my husband who was very unstable emotionally.

I did not go to any college tours with my daughter. I knew if I went my husband would talk badly about me in front of her and this would make her feel very sad.

I took my real-estate exam and did not pass it. I know my husband will be calling me more names, and I feel so badly for not passing it. I was hoping I could make some money, enjoy working with him, or do something that I know he wanted me to do. One of my college friends told me there is a job opening for a night shift therapist at this non-profit agency. The hours are 10 PM to 6 AM and a BA in Psychology is good enough. It would be 5 nights a week, and the pay was $500 a week. I got happy! I was desperate. I told my husband and he asked when are you starting. I talked to a few of my friends whose opinions I respect. None of them like the idea. They all agreed my sleep is important, and there would be other jobs. I prayed to God and begged Him for answers. I think He gave me answers through all the negative responses I got with my friends. So I denied the job offer, but lied to my husband and told him they did not want me. I thought about my son waking up in the middle of the night with a nightmare and I would not be around to make him feel safe. I knew I could trust my husband to be there for my son, but I do not think my son would even go to my husband for comfort. He lost the hope of getting comfort from his father when he was almost 3 years old. He told me on one of our individual times together that he hates his father because his father yells a lot, makes me and his sister cry a lot, and he smoke cigarettes.

Over all I am feeling sad, worried, and weak. He is not putting enough money in our bank account. I have been using my credit card for almost everything. He told me today he will not pay off my credit card and "I need to get a fucking job as soon as possible." He looked at me today and said, "Why don't you go to Sunset Blvd. and prostitute? You have the looks and the body. Make it useful."

7/24/2005

I took my baby girl to her college. Although it wasn't starting for 6 more weeks, she had to go and stay for a whole week for orientation and experience the college life. She was very happy I could tell she cannot wait to get out of this home and never look back again. Her eyes were sparkling with joy and I loved looking at them.

We did not talk a lot in the car ride, just listened to music. While I was driving I kept having different snap shots of all the joy she has brought to my life. The first time I saw her eyes I thought it was the most magical set of God's masterpiece. I kept crying, talking to God, and saying wow, she is too beautiful. Although I was in labor for 36 hours, the minute I met her eyes I felt energized, with no more pain in my body and all was good. She was born in the wintertime, so maybe that is the reason that she keeps carrying all this warmth anywhere she goes. Her entering my cold, lonely life was one of God's most outstanding miracles in my life. Staring at her just takes me to the gratitude mood. I kept seeing how hard her life has been because she was born to me and my husband. Why didn't she have a normal, stable peaceful life at home? Why, why, and so many more why's. I had no answers. I was just proud to be her mother.

When we arrived at the college, she asked me to drop her off. I asked if she wanted me to help her with her stuff and she said no. I knew she was dying to get out of the car and be with her friends. I just hugged her, kissed her head, and told her God had answered her prayers because she is in her dream college. Now it was her turn to make God and herself proud. She hugged me back, told me she loves me, and she will see me next Sunday. I did not cry in front of her, but the minute she left I cried all the way until I was in my garage. I cried for all those bad memories she had in her beautiful mind. I cried for being a weak mother, and for not having the backbone to protect her from her father's ongoing verbal abuse. I was sorry that she had witnessed so many bad scenes from our kitchen table that some of her new friends at college would never get to see it in their whole life. I was sorry for taking her to day care when she was only one year old for eight hours a day so I could go to beauty school. I was sorry for not being next to her on Saturday mornings since she was one year old until she was 12 years old. Every Saturday I had to work early in the morning at beauty salon as that was the busiest day because all the working people wanted to get their hair done then. I was sorry for not protecting her as much as I should have, but I knew for sure I was very happy to be her mother.

I cannot wait for the summer school to end. I will have two weeks off. I am going to just take my son to some museums. He loves art work and taking pictures. We will go to the beach and he wants to see Catalina Island for a day. My husband told me we cannot go on any summer vacations. I am sad, but fine with it. I just cannot wait for the hunting season to start. That would be a real vacation.

9/20/2005

I am going to school at night time and trying to get my daughter ready for her college. She has some last minutes shopping to do. I have no money since he has not deposited any money into our joint account plus he is gone hunting. I am trying so hard not to cry in front of my daughter. I feel sad, weak, hopeless, and powerless. I checked my husband's bank accounts today. I found out he has $8800 in his savings account and $4500 in his own personal checking account. I prayed and asked God to show me a way today to have some money to do the last minute shopping for my baby girl. Wow! God is great! I went to bank, took $300 cash from his saving, and deposited $800 from his checking into our joint checking account. I came home and told my daughter let's go get your stuff. I did not feel bad or guilty at all. I know he will be devastated, but these days he is devastated about why I made his coffee too dark or too sweet. He calls me a useless whore, a loser, and a hopeless bitch. He cusses at my dead father at least once a day. So with all these ongoing shows in my house, a few more after he finds out is not going to kill me. He will be back in 3 to 4 days, and as soon as he is home we are going to move my daughter to college. I am very sure he will know about this after she is gone. Having said all this, I was very sad in my heart. I was going to do hair again, and knowing my sweet son will be home alone with him on Saturdays and three nights a week was terrifying. I needed to do something to make some money.

While I was looking at bed covers with my daughter, my mind was worrying about how am I going to finish my grad school. How am I going to handle all this? Maybe I should just divorce him today, but I realized I just cannot. I have no money, no family, and of course no backbone. I prayed to God that he would die on his hunting trip.

10/30/2005

I am doing hair 20 hours a week. I do not have too many clients since I lost almost all of them when I stopped five years ago. So I have been sitting around a lot, praying, talking to God, and actually doing my homework. Home is the same. He is very mad at me for not making a lot of money. I have my own account, he has his own, and we have our joint. He told me I cannot use the joint account at all, and I need to make money, put it in my own account, and use only that. I had tried to explain to him I am not making a lot of money, and he had told me that is just my own problem. I am heartbroken. I do not know what to do. I keep talking to God. I know he will take care of all this. I am grateful for my health, my amazing kids, and my family and friends.

Last week I had such an amazing experience at school that I will never forget, and I thanked God so many times for His love and help. I have a class about couples counseling. The person who is teaching class is the head of the admissions for this master's degree program. He is the one who denied my application twice, and finally met with me and I asked him to give me a chance to enter the program and he did. It is the same class that my hair client was studying for 10 years ago, the book for the class was couple in crisis. He even complimented me last week after our group discussion. He told me I will be an amazing therapist. He thanked me for meeting with him in person two years ago, and convincing him to let me be part of this program. I have been getting A's or high B's. I love studying and learning how to connect with people in pain. I am learning to connect with my own pain more and am trying to grow in this process. I came home that night and I cried and thanked God for making my dreams come true, one at a time, in His own timing. I am proud to be a graduate student in the field of marriage and family therapy. Thank you, God!

12/06/2005

I am not looking forward to the holidays. It is so hard to wait around in the beauty salon for new walk-in clients, while I feel guilty for not being home with my son. He needs me and I hardly get to see him. He is having a hard time being with his father. If I knew my husband would force me to work while I was in graduate school, I would not do this. I feel selfish and hopeless at the same time. Why is it my eight-year old son's fault that his mom is getting educated, while his father is hunting and doing anything his heart desires? My husband lied to me. In 2003 he told me I should have the 3rd child, or work, or go to grad school. I thought we were clear about all this.

Anyway, he decided to pay my credit card bill last month which was almost $15,000. He said it would affect my credit and his credit because we are married. I still hate him and wish he were dead. He was so mad at me yesterday because I did not have money to pay for our dinner. He decided to take me and my son out. After they gave us the bill he handed it to me and I told him I did not have cash. He called me stupid and said he is tired of feeding me. My son was sitting there too. I did not say anything. I just wished he were dead.

With this ongoing crisis in my personal daily life, I have lost my desire for school. I actually feel guilty about going and my mind is all over the place. I am praying God will help me do the right thing.

Today I cried while I was taking my shower. I do not know how long I was crying. Then my husband started to yell and cuss at me, telling me stop wasting money like that. He hates it when I take long showers. After my shower got interrupted, I just sat on the floor and cried more. I asked God to kill me today. It would be the best thing that could happen to me. I wanted to be far from my husband. I have been praying God would take away his life, but I respect God's wishes. He is not ready to take my husband's life yet. So today, dear God, please end my life. I am tired of failing in front of my kids. I am tired of all the daily struggles. I want to join my father in heaven. Thank you, dear God, for everything.

Everything was pretty much the same for the next few months. I was praying every day that God would just make my daily struggles easier. God did not kill me. I was alive, pushing through the storm.

My mother came in February. It was not a good idea with the ongoing problems in our home, but she said she wanted to be there for my son. She also wanted to help with the daily household chores. Her intentions were great, but my husband overall did not like any of my family. He loved the idea that I was thousands of miles away from my support system. My poor mother tried very hard to create some kind of peace in my household, but it was just out of her hands. Every morning she made tea and breakfast for my husband. She cooked, cleaned, and even did gardening. You need to know something about my mother. She hates doing house chores. When my father was alive and was in the army, we had a full time house keeper. My mother cooked our meals and gave us love and attention. She is a very social person. When she comes to visit it is very hard for her since she does not speak the language. She does not drive so depends on me to take her places.

My husband was fine with her for few days, and then he started to be mean to her by not saying hello or just ignoring her. In my culture the elder must be respected by the younger people. So he knew exactly what to do to hurt her feelings. Then at the dinner table a few times he called me names, put me down, and told my poor mother that I am a useless piece of meat. It was nasty. He told my son to call me donkey, and call my mother big donkey. My son, who was only 10 years old, told him he is a donkey and his mother is a big donkey. He got mad, took off his belt, and went after my son. My poor mother was crying. I told him to stop all this nonsense. He got mad at me and went after me with his belt. He hit my legs while I was running. My mother started to scream and told him to stop all this. She told him to stop hurting her baby. He yelled at my poor old mother who was shaking and told her to "go to hell with your fucking useless whore daughter."

My son was still running around the house. It was bad. I just wanted him to stop talking, and go somewhere far. I was talking to God and asking for help. Right at this time our next door neighbor, who was friends with my husband, came over to talk to my husband. I wanted to hug him and thank him for coming, but I just invited him inside and asked him if he would like some tea. He stayed for a long time, God bless him.

My poor mother was shaking and told me she is going to call her friend in Los Angeles and have her come over tomorrow to take her to their home. She told me she was worried about me. She told me what just happened was not normal, and if my husband was not afraid of the law I would have lots of bruises on my body. I agreed. I told her I hate my husband and I started to cry. I told her I was mad at her for arranging this marriage for me. She cried and said she was sorry. I told her I wanted to divorce him, but I didn't have the money to pay for a divorce. Also emotionally I was not ready with the school, my two internships, and my kids. My mother cried and told me she will try to help me, but she was still shaking.

My son woke up and came crying to me. He said, "Mom, do not divorce him because in this country the father would get 50 percent custody of the child. Please wait until I am 18". Oh my heavenly Father, I felt like I was in the middle of an earthquake.

The next day my sister called and after my mother told her what had happened, my sister told my mother she needed to come back to Iran as soon as possible. She made the arrangements and got her ticket confirmed to leave in the next two days. When my husband heard all this, he felt badly I guess. He decided to play one of his sick games on my poor mother. While my mother was trying to pack her stuff, he told her she needs to give him back my four gold rings. He told me in front of my mother that he had seen her hide my gold rings and my mother is a thief. Oh my dear God, I just looked at him and felt sorry for him. I had no idea how sick he was. To make the show more interesting he took my car keys and told me he will not let me take my mother to the airport. He was very serious. I was frozen. I looked at my poor mother and we both started to cry.

He left and we just sat and cried some more. My mother kept telling me she would never steal anything from anybody and this is just very sick. I hold her I am so sorry for this mess. She called her friend in Los Angeles and asked her to come pick her up right away, although her flight was in two days. Her friend came. I felt so small. I just wanted to die. I was ashamed to see how my mother was leaving my house. I just told her I am so sorry. She left and I cried all day. I just wanted to die.

My husband came home and smiled when my son said grandma is gone and it was his fault. The next few days I started to look around his office and yes, I found my four gold rings under his file cabinet. I was so mad. I called Iran and told my poor mother that I found the rings in his office. She cried and said oh my God, he is very sick.

In the middle of all this, I got a job as a case manager. One of my classmates told me about it. She knew the person who was interviewing, and she had put in a good word for me. I told my friend I had no experience with office or computer work, but I knew how to work with people. I also told her I can connect with people very easily.

I went for the interview the next day. I was offered the job after 10 minutes. The manager told me she liked how I had no experience, and they needed fresh blood so they could train people the way they wanted. The good thing about the job was I would make some steady money at $15 an hour. That same day they wanted some personal information like my social security number. I called home and told my husband I need my social security card. He kept all my personal documents in his home office. He told me I should call him my master, and he said never forget who is your master. I just ignored him. I was so happy because it was a steady source of income. I would get a pay check every 2 weeks. The other good part was getting some exposure with office work. I needed something to put in my future resume. The best part is I would be working 3 days a week. I liked that too, but the first 3 months was training and I had to go every day. It was hard, but I liked working with older adults, trying to help them look for jobs, or overall helping them to get some volunteer work. I loved connecting with all of them. I had to learn a lot of office skills and made some good friends.

I kept hair dressing for a while too. I was so busy. The worst part was the guilty feeling that I had toward my sweet loving son. I missed his beautiful eyes while I was gone. For three months I was gone six days a week. I kept doing hair on Saturdays plus the two nights of me being away for school was just hard on him. The hatred for my husband increased more and more because he was not working at all. He would just watch TV for hours, sit in the back yard, and cuss at life and me anytime he felt like it. I kept asking God for peace every day. I begged God to take care of my son while I was gone and protect him against my husband's bad angry behaviors. I was not even talking to my husband since the incident occurred with my poor mother.

3/26/2006

I got up very early and went to gym. I love the relaxing feeling that I always have after a workout. I came home, got ready, and prepared my son ready for his soccer game. Today I did not have any hair clients until noon. So it is a treat being able to take my son to his game. I love spending time with him. I feel very blessed to be his mother.

My husband was sleeping downstairs in the family room in front of the TV. We were trying to leave, but he just woke up. He started yelling at me and my son. He asked my son why he didn't tell him he had a game today. I told him we forgot. We left and I was worried he may come after us and create a show. Thank God, I think he just went back to sleep.

We went to the game. My son was holding my hand while I was driving. He kept telling me how happy he was to be with me, and I told him I love him more than my life. I told him I was sorry for not being at home more. He cried and he said he knew I was trying to make money for him and he was very proud of me for going to school. I told him as soon as I get my degree I will be around more and we could do so much together. He told me since he was three years old he hated his father because he knew his father was mean to me. Oh my dear God, this felt very heavy on my heart. I started to cry and could not stop. I just kept telling him I was sorry and I wish I could bring him to a normal loving home. I cried more. I had to stop the car. He held my hands and told me stop saying you are sorry. You are making me cry now. So I quietly prayed more, asked God to help me to pull it together and help me to get him to his soccer game.

We got there. He was happy to be with his friends. I was just sad. I sat and tried to watch the game. While my body was sitting there, my mind was miles away. I was thinking about the phone call that not only changed my life forever, but changed my sweet boy's life too. I started to just feel hopeless again.

Dustin, my son's friend's father, came and sat next to me. He looked at me and said not worry that everything is going to be fine. He said my heart felt heavy to him, and since he was sitting next to me he felt the pain in my heart. Then he asked where my husband was. I started to cry as soon as he asked about him. I told him a lot of things. I just needed to talk and he wanted to listen. I cried and apologized to him for telling him all this. He said let's pray together. He asked God to bring more peace and clarity to my heart. He praised me for doing all the things I was doing, and he complimented me on how hard I was trying to be a good mother to my son. He told me he and his wife met 15 years ago in high school and got married 10 years ago. They have four kids and they moved here because he had a job transfer. He said his wife was missing her family in New York, and this makes him feel very sad. He said he told his work that he needs to move back home as soon as the school year is over. Then he had tears in his eyes. He told me he is very sorry that I have been separated from my family, my support system, for the last 18 years. He said he is so sorry that my husband is so mean to me and my kids. He said he promised my season will come. God had good plans for me and my children. He told me just hang in there, you are doing great. He finished by saying my son is the only boy on the soccer team whom he likes his son to play with because my son is polite, kind, and fun. Then he said thanks to God and you for being such a good mother. He held my hands and prayed for me. I felt so relaxed. I felt like I just lost 100 pounds. I told him I will never forget all his kind words. It feels great when you feel heard. I just thanked God for this wonderful conversation. I needed it. Thank you, Lord.

5/17/2006

I have been thinking about my life. I am very mad at what my husband did to my poor mother. First he tried to beat me up in front of her, then hid my gold rings and accused her of stealing them, almost kicking her out of our home. I looked in the mirror in my bathroom while I was getting ready and I saw a hopeless, powerless woman. I just felt disgusted. I looked around the room and realized I am just a stranger to this room, this home, and this crappy contract that is called marriage, or make that jail. I started to pray, and then the tears came. I told God if this is what my life is like then I want to die. I cried more and ended up falling asleep while I was crying. I had a dream about my two kids. We were walking together, just the three of us. We all looked happy, relaxed, and free. I was in the middle of them and they both were holding to my hands tightly. We were walking in a big park full of trees and it was hot.

I woke up and talked to God more. I told him I do not want to die. I love my kids and they need me. I decided to just go and do some basic shopping for the house. For some strange reason I passed all the different aisles in the store, and I ended up finding myself in front of some big suitcases. I called my husband and told him I am not coming home. I will come home to pick up my son and my clothes. Then I was going to either a shelter for abused woman and children or maybe I would go to a motel. He got quiet which was very different from his usual cussing and screaming. I think he got the point that I was really serious. He started to cry on the phone and begged me to come home. He said he will go stay with his family if I need space. He kept saying he loves me and he doesn't want to lose me.

I said with a very cold voice, "You lost me when our daughter was only few weeks old when you slapped me on my face after I left my purse at that wedding. That was 18 years ago." He kept saying he knows he had made a lot of mistakes, but I should not do anything right now because I am under a lot of stress from school, work, internship, and trying to raise my son.

My response was, "You just now realized how stressful my life is? You are the one who started all this ongoing stress in my life!" I was crying at this point and told him I was working as a hair dresser and he kept putting me down, calling me names, and kind of forced me to go to school while he decided he had so many different interests in life like hunting, skiing, and did not really like to work anymore. "You forced me to work six days a week while I was in school. You took my son's childhood away from me. Do you know I cry on my way to school at night, because I miss his beautiful eyes? Do you know every minute he is with you I am worried and feel guilty about how your abusive, mean language would not only impact my son's life, but it will affect his children's lives too? So just stay away from me and my son. I will be home in 20 minutes. I will move out. I am not sure where I would go, but I will call the police if you try to stop me, and I really mean it."

Oh my dear God, I had no idea where those words came from, but they did. I came home with two big suitcases. I went upstairs and started to pack my stuff. Then I realized I needed to talk to my son and prepare him. All this time my husband was downstairs, out of my sight, just as I asked. I went to my son's room, hugged him, kissed his big beautiful eyes, and told him we are going away for a little while. He wanted to know if we were taking a road trip. I said no. We are going to a motel. He asked if we could take our dog. I said no, most motels do not let animals stay. In the back of my head I am thinking about shelters for abused woman and children and what the policy about animals was there.

I did about 120 hours of internship in a shelter for abused women and children before I got my BA in Psychology around 2002. I am sure it sounds ironic, but I did it. I helped abused women go to court and get restraining orders from the abusive husbands, while I was living in a five- bedroom home worth over a million dollars, driving a convertible Mercedes Benz, and I envied their courage. I praised them for their strength, and I hated myself for staying in my loveless, abusive marriage. I kept telling myself I do not want my children to grow up in a broken divorced family. Well, the truth is, they are living with their broken hearts in a family that has been broken for over a decade.

While I am thinking about all this I just remember the "A" grade that I got in that internship. My supervisor wrote on my final paper that she was impressed how I was able to function just great at the time of crisis. She wrote my ability to stay calm and peaceful, but at the same time being able to use my mind to do what I had to do, was very special. She wrote that I was able to disconnect from my emotions and act very rational. She said these qualities will make me an amazing therapist. Oh my dear God, I had news for her. I was just dying to tell her this is my daily life. Welcome to my world of ongoing crisis.

I came out of my deep thinking when I heard my son crying. He kept saying he wants to pack only if we are able to take our dog and also if we could go Grand Canyon. Then he said he didn't want to miss any of school as he wanted to get the perfect attendance award at the end of the school year. He asked if we could take our vacation in four weeks when his school was out. I just looked at him, held him, kissed him at least 10 times, and told him we do not have to go anywhere today without our dog and he does not have to miss school. I just could not do this to him. He was not ready for more changes in his life, or maybe I just used this as an excuse because I was not ready.

I went downstairs. My husband started to cry. He said he was very sorry that I came to a point of leaving him. He said he would call my mother right now, apologize to her for accusing her of stealing my gold and kicking her out of our home. He actually did call right away and talked to her for a while.

Then I told him I do not love him, I don't want to grow old with him, and I do not want to do anything with him. I told him let's just live together like roommates and let's raise our son together. Let's try to give him a family and a normal life. I told him I will not leave tonight because my son is not ready. I also told him if he raises his hand on me or my son I will call the police. I meant it. He looked at me and said he understood.

5/21/06

My husband's brother called me and invited me to go to his parent's home for a family meeting about the marital problems with my husband. I really respect my brother-in-law. He is very kind, smart, and when he asked me to go, I agreed and went to my in-law's home.

It was such a powerful experience for me. I prayed God would be in charge and be my voice. Oh, He was my voice. I had an out-of-body experience. I could not believe it was me talking like that.

His mother never admitted her son had any problems. She looked at me and asked me if I was planning to leave as soon as I got my master's degree. I always admire how smart this woman is. If she had come to the United States when she was younger, she would have done a lot with her life. I always admired her strength and the ongoing love she has for her children. She had helped me many, many days and nights when her son was not available to take care of our kids. She is an amazing devoted grandmother, and while I am alive I will always be thankful for every loving moment she has spent with my kids.

Before I answered her question I asked God for her forgiveness and understanding. Then I just told her and all of them the whole truth. I said I do not love your son anymore. I am tired of walking on eggshells, and if he touches me or my kids I will call the police. I told them I am not the naive, 19 year-old girl I once was. I am a 39 year-old mother. I have changed and grown. I am working six days a week and go to school two nights a week, while my husband is relaxing--watching TV or going on hunting, hiking, or on skiing trips. I am trying to teach my son some life lessons. I am trying to teach him good values, and I believe he still likes his father. So to answer the question if I am planning to get a divorce right after my school is over, the answer is yes, unless your son changes. I also added if my son loves him enough that he cannot be without him I will stay. I will work two or even three jobs and will take care of our family. I said all I am asking is for him to try to be a good father to our son and stop being mean all the time.

They just looked at me and said thank you for coming. My husband told his parents he will try to do what he has to do to keep his family because he loves his family. We thanked my brother- in-law for his time. We left. We came home. I went upstairs and he slept downstairs. I thanked God again for my courage to be open and honest.

Things were more peaceful at home for only a few days. He simply got tired of faking being good. He at least tried, by coming to the grocery store and trying to carry the grocery bags from the car into the house, which was very out of his comfort zone, he cooked dinner three nights while I was at school. Although the food was really bad, I thanked him for trying. He took showers more than once a week and changed his clothes.

7/28/2006

Bad, bad, bad, day. He just lost it again. He hit me with his head. The whole story started when we were invited to his sister's house for a dinner party that she had planned one week ago. She decided to invite us at the last minute. Well, I had homework to do. My kids were relaxing by the pool and were happy to be home. He said we all should go in the next 30 minutes. I told him I am enjoying being with the kids at home and in a little while I needed to do my homework. I was not in a mood all those people for 4 to 6 hours. He got mad, started to cuss, and hit me. Next he went to my son and told him to get out of the pool now. He then told my 18 year old college student daughter to get ready. She told him she does not feel like going. He got mad, took the car keys from me, and told her she needs to be in the car or she will pay for it.

Then he started running after my ten year old son. My son was crying and asking me for help. I held my son. He was shaking. I started to shake. We looked at each other. Then I saw my beautiful daughter's eyes were filled with tears. I started to pray in my head. I had one of those one-on-one conversations with my Beloved God. I asked him to show me a way out now. In my head I was thinking, come on, do something. Call the police, get rid of him now. On the other hand, I was hearing not yet. Not yet.

Then I changed and helped my kids to get ready. I held my son in my arms while I was putting his shirt on. He started to cry again. I told him, "I will take care of you. I will leave him, and I will do my best to have full custody of you. We are going to put all of this behind us. I will just hang in there and pray to God."

We went to the party, which was a waste of time. I was sitting there, but my mind was miles away. I was having one of those daydreams in my head. I started imagining life without him. In my dreams I was traveling with my kids. We were in Hawaii around Christmas time because there was this giant Christmas tree in the middle of our hotel. Then the next day we were swimming in the ocean and all of a sudden it started to rain. We were laughing and swimming in the ocean under amazing rain. It was just a magical trip. He was not with us.

Well the next year was very hard. I am sure you are wondering what is new. It was my last year of grad school. Part of the program for graduation was to have 250 of hours direct client contact. I started to see clients two nights a week in this amazing nonprofit organization. I loved the one-on-one experience with all my clients. The whole experience was just breath-taking for me. I liked the classes too. This year of training was very focused on personal growth, discovering the real reasons why I am in this field, and learning to create healthy boundaries with the clients and overall in my personal life.

One thing I learned this year was that I saw myself and my problems in almost all my clients. I felt blessed to be able to experience so many loses in my life. I know today God wanted me to become tender, compassionate, and caring. I worked three days a week as a case manager and did hair on Saturdays. My marriage was very bad and I was drifting away more and more from my husband. I still felt very sad and guilty for not being home with my son, but I had no other choices.

I cried one night after class, talked to one of my professors very briefly, and asked her for advice. She told me looks like you are done being a doormat. Your inner voice is getting stronger. She said divorce is very hard because she had gone through it five years prior. She told me if you go for it now, you may have to stop school, since divorce and grad school are very demanding, so it is your decision. I thanked her and I decided to finish school and also try to stay optimistic, praying he would change. But he just got worse.

4/18/2007

God, please help me to have peace in my life. God, you are the light in my darkness. I am nothing without you. Please be here with me right now and keep me going. I do not know what you have in store for me, but I know I am in your hands and you will take care of me. Dear God, thank you for all the growing pains.

Sometimes I have a hard time stopping myself from crying when my clients are crying, but today in class my professor was talking about how a client/therapist relationship could be like a parent/child relationship as far as protecting and holding them. Her example was when your child is crying because he or she fell down and has bruises all over the body, the last thing your child needs is for you to fall apart and start crying. I will try to always remember this. I need to stay calm, and strong. Sometimes I cry for my clients while I am driving and then I start praying for them.

The worst part is two nights a week I have to see clients until 9:00 pm. When I get home I have too much on my mind that I cannot sleep. I try to spend some time with my sweet, loving son, before he falls asleep. Oh my dear God, I love him so much! I miss him like crazy, but I feel trapped with school stuff. I want my divorce and his freedom, but I need to finish school, get a job, find financial stability, and go on with my kids.

Anyway, when I have a lot in my head at nighttime, I start cooking food for my son and my husband's meals for the next day since I won't be home. I like to make sure they have home-cooked food. I love mixing all the different spices, fresh herbs, and fresh vegetables together. Cooking is very healing to my soul. I would love to write a cooking book one day, and share all my secrets. All my family and friends tell me my cooking is very unique because I don't follow a recipe at all. I use whatever we have at home and a whole meal takes me 30 to 45 minutes to prepare.

Anyway, I also work out every single day in the morning around 5:30am. I like to go to the gym before my busy day starts. I want to make sure I take care of myself so I won't get burned out in this field.

Self-care is another thing we talked about in class today. Journaling my feelings has been helping me to get rid of the clutter in my head. Sometimes I ask God to give me the energy or courage I need to be able to see my next clients.

Overall this year is just busy, but I am happy to finally start to see the light at the end of the tunnel. I have amazing days and sparkling moments with my clients. The only problem is I need to see more clients in the next 4 weeks and this organization has too many interns.

So today I called one of my professors from last year. I asked him if he had any ideas where I could intern and get more hours. It is amazing how my beloved God works. The professor told me he just got promoted in his job and he is the supervisor for this program. He told me to meet with him today. Well, I met with him in his office. He told me he will do all the paperwork, and have me start my internship as early as next week. I cried. I don't know if it was tears from joy or my deep pain in my heart. All he asked was how bad everything was. I told him bad, very bad. He told me he will help me to rewrite my resume. He also he told me, "I am here for you and I really mean that." He told me he is very proud of my strength and courage. His last words were, "You will be using all this pain and growth with your clients." So I feel better today. I know, my dear God, you are guiding me through life. I thank you again for blessing me with all your love. I am sorry for being sad and depressed at the beginning of this journal entry. I feel so much better now. Thank you, dear God, for more peaceful days to come.

4/23/07

I need to forgive, forget, and move on. I am keeping too much anger and negativity inside of me. God, please release all my anger and redirect my energy to a positive flow. I know negative thinking creates negative behaviors, and negative behaviors create negative actions. Today is what it is and I need to face it. There is no use in fighting it. I am very thankful, dear God, for today, and only today. But sometimes I cannot stop thinking about what had happened yesterday, and the day before, and all the sad yesterdays.

He took the car keys and left for the soccer game with my sweet son. Four months ago I decided to sign him up to be a coach for our son's soccer team. I prayed about it, and told myself this would be good for three reasons: 1) it would make him shower, change and do something productive with his life that could help with his low self-esteem and depressed mood. My husband loves soccer and has been playing it since he was a child, so in my head he should be a pro. 2) It would give the father and son something to talk about and share. 3) It would be good for my son to see how his father is so talented in this sport and would make my son feel proud about his father. So when he saw the papers that he was the head coach it was almost three months later, and way too late to change the situation. See, with my husband I have learned he would do well when he is in a done situation. After he saw his name as the head coach, he was not happy. He started yelling and cussing for few minutes, but he knew there was nothing he could do. It was too late.

So my plans worked for a while. He would take showers, change, and take my son to the practices. Sometimes I could hear them talking about all the soccer stuff in the garage while they were walking inside. My son even told me he had no idea how good his father is in soccer. Then things changed when the games started. He was in the worst mood after his team lost the two games in the last two weeks. He just cannot take it.

I am regretting my decision even more today. He carries the loss until the next game. The bad news is I have a feeling they may never win any games, because the players are just not into soccer at all. So yesterday they had a game. My son was so happy that I was going to go with them and watch the game. My husband got mad at me in the morning after I made him breakfast. He already had two cups of coffee, so I turned the coffeemaker off. He wanted more, so he got up and when he saw the coffee make was off, he just lost it. He started to cuss, calling me an ignorant whore in front of my son. I just left the kitchen.

The next thing I heard was my son crying and the garage door closing. I started to cry. I prayed to God he wouldn't hit my son in the car. I looked for my car keys and sure enough he took them. I called him and told him I wanted to watch my son's game and why did he leave without me? Where is the other car key? He said, "Fuck off, you mother fucker".

Then I heard my son's voice saying, "Daddy, please, let's go home and pick up my mom." Then he hung up the phone. I cried loudly then I prayed, asking God to show me a way. I called one of my best friend's whose son was in the soccer game, told her my husband took my keys, yes accidentally , and wondered if she could pick me up. She did, and I made it to the game. Thank you, God!

Well, they lost the game. He got very mad. He told my son he had to watch the next game so he could learn how to play better. It was already 2:30 pm. He was hungry, I was hungry, we did not have lunch, but my husband did not care. He said that's too bad because we are going to watch the next game. He showed the car keys to me and my son. He said just shut up and watch the game. My son started to cry. I held him and told him I was so sorry. Then I started cry too. It was so hard to stop.

After he finished watching the game it was almost 4:00 pm. My son called him a bad father since he forced us to sit and watch this game against our wills. My son started to cry, and said to my husband he wished his father was dead and he was a fatherless child. By this time we were in the car and he was driving. My son started to cry. He was very hungry and tired. He told his father to just go home so he could have his lunch at 4:45. My husband lost it badly. He drove to the parking lot of a business center, and since it was Sunday nobody was there. He parked the car, opened his door, got out of the car, and took the dog's leash out. He looked at my son and said, "I will show you what a bad father is. You talk too much, just like your fucking mother". My poor son was speechless. He was in shock. Then he started running in the parking lot. I started to cry, pray, and scream all at the same time. I don't know how I did it all, but I did. I asked my dear God to help. By this time he said we both must say sorry right away or he would kill us. My son and I said sorry to him, and I thanked God when he sat in the car and told us "fucking assholes" to get in the car. We got home and I just took some food upstairs to my son. We stayed in his room for the rest of the night. It felt safe to be away from him.

Dear God please bring some peace to my life and my children's lives. God, I am opening my heart to you all the way. Please direct me. I am keeping my faith.

This was the time I was counting down days for my graduation. I was praying sometimes 5 to 10 times a day for God just to be with me, holding me throughout the storm. I had some nights that I cried in my car after finishing with my last client. I would just cry, and ask God to bless me with enough energy so I could manage to drive home.

The day of my 40th birthday I worked from 8:00 am to 2:30 pm. I picked up my son from his school, brought him home, gave him some food, went to my school, and then went to my internship. So I got home around 9:30 PM and my husband asked me, "Where have you been fucking around at this time?" I just looked at him and prayed in my head dear God, I need you to keep him far from me, and bless me with some peace. I was so tired, physically and emotionally had nothing to offer him. I just wanted to look at my son's beautiful eyes, where I could see God's miracles, and I did.

5/18/2007
11:37 PM

I am very happy and thankful to God for everything. Tomorrow is less than 12 hours away. I will be done with school. Thank you, God. It has been my dream to get educated. I feel very strong. Dear God, I am nothing without you. Thank you for all the love and protection. Please keep guiding me. I am ending my job as a case manager and I am not going to do hair anymore. Dear God, with your help I have a master's degree. I want to use it and try to get jobs that are strongly related to my degree. I am just so happy and grateful, dear God.

5/20/07

Thank you, God, for everything. I thank you for all your miracles in my life. I am speechless. I am nothing without you. I graduated yesterday. I cannot believe it happened. I had one of the best days in my life. Dear God, thank you for giving me the will power.

The Breakthrough

My supervisor, who at my internship called me and told me the agency is going to hire me since I speak Farsi, and they need someone who could help Farsi speaking clients. Dear God, I am so thankful! I have a job now. I was told I could start in two weeks, as soon as they finish all the background check. I am very happy. None of my friends got hired by the agency that they did their internship with. I know for sure it is all you. You know how bad I needed a job. I am grateful for my hair dressing days and case managing days. They are behind me and I am ready to work as a marriage and family therapist intern in two weeks or it may be sooner. I pray that you would use me to carry your love to all my clients. I pray you will use me to bring out their best. I pray you would bring some peace and stability into my life. Dear God, yesterday I did not even want to see my husband at my graduation. I have been hurt by him so deeply that in happy days like my graduation day, I just did not want to see him.

It was sad that I just remembered what he did two weeks ago. It was a Saturday, so I went to the beauty salon and worked from 8:00 to 1:00. I was happy to go home and be with my son, make him lunch, play games, take him to the park, or invite his friends over so they could play. While I was driving I decided to stop at the grocery store and get a few items for lunch. I got home with my groceries and started to make lunch. My son told me he had not had breakfast yet because his father was sleeping, just woke up, and had been on the phone. I got sad, but kept making his lunch. My husband came to the kitchen and told me the dog was hungry too. I ignored him, but started to cook some chicken for the dog too. Then I gave my son his food.

My husband came from the backyard to the kitchen, took my son's food, and went out to the backyard. My son started to cry and told his father he took the food that was for him. My husband got mad, slapped my son, and threw away his food. I got so mad I asked him what was wrong with him. Why did he take his son's food? He looked at me and told me I was not at work all day. He told me he knew I was fucking around because when he called the beauty salon, he was told I was not there. I did try to explain to him I stopped at the grocery store. He got madder and by this time my son was still crying for his food that he took away. I looked at my husband and told him to please calm down. I was not in a mood to create more fighting. I told him I was sorry that he was hungry and to give me 15 minutes I would prepare his lunch too.

He said, "Fuck you. Why do you talk to me like I am sick?" Then he pushed me to the backyard. My son came after me. My husband locked the backyard door and left the house. I could not believe this. He did not come home until 11:30 pm.

At first I was in denial about how I have been in my last 20 years of marriage. Then my son got really sad, and told me, "Mom, why did he do this to us? I am hot, I want water, and I am hungry. Call the police, Mom. Please call the police. Have him arrested. He cannot do this to us."

I started to cry, held him, told him I am so sorry, and maybe I should call the police. Then I realized he took away my cell phone when I got home from work, which was very normal for him to do. In the last few months he checked my emails and my cell phone very often. I did not like it, but I had no energy to fight with him.

So my son and I had to stay in the backyard for almost eight hours. I told him let's just swim with our clothes on. We pretended we were in Hawaii, it was raining, and we were swimming in the ocean while it was raining. My son liked the game. He said we needed to use the water hose so that could be the rain. We did, and thanked God for the fruit trees in the backyard so we had something to eat until the he came home.

When he got home he told us we have to apologize to him first and then he would let us go in. We were so tired we did say sorry to him and went upstairs.

It is sad that I remembered all these things on the day of my graduation. Too bad because all I wanted was to have a day filled with love and joy.

The Breakthrough

He came and he gave me flowers. I looked at him and just cried. If my tears could talk these would be their words: "If you touch me or my lovely children one more time, I will call the police. Do not mess up with me anymore. I am an educated mother, who is 40 years old. I will go all the way if I have to in order to create a safe, peaceful life for my 11 year old son. I just have a feeling I will no longer be with you because you will never change. You will hurt me and my son more and more and more, so good-bye."

5/25/2007
7:30 AM

I am sitting here at the medical office trying to get my physical examination done for my job. Yesterday I did the bi-lingual testing. I had to write a letter in Farsi to an imaginary client, and then I had to explain my treatment plans for the team in Farsi and English. My dear God, I have a good feeling about it. The new supervisor talked to me on the phone and said since they need me, they are willing to keep the job for me until end of August. Then he said they want me to start working now and will hire me right away. If I am tired I should take some time out, relax, call back in two months, and hopefully the job would still be there. But they may give the job to someone else that is qualified while I am relaxing. So the bottom line is he told me is he cannot guarantee me the job will be there if I take two months off. I told my husband that I am tired, would prefer to spend this summer with our kids, and take the job in two months. I even cried. I almost begged him to allow me enjoy this summer with my son, take him to beach, invite his friends to a pool party at our home, and just be with him because I miss him and am tired. I added that if I start work I cannot take any time off for almost a year. Of course he told me to shut up and stop talking nonsense. Start the job as soon as you can. When I told him how much my monthly income would be, he sat down in the kitchen table. He took his calculator out and put some numbers in there. Then he said that is not enough. You must make more money. Our monthly expenses are more, so start looking for a job on Saturdays too. I just looked at him and in my heart I wished him dead. I actually prayed he would die today. Well, dear God, I am so thankful I got this job. I know you will bless me with energy to do what I have to do. I am grateful for all the love and blessings you have given me. Thank you.

6/22/2007

My 21st anniversary was two days ago. It is so hard to be in a loveless, cold abusive relationship for more than two decades. Shame on me, just shame on me. I do not know why I am here, and I am not sure how much longer I can live like this. Thank you, my dear God, for helping me to push through the storm.

Last Sunday I asked one of my friends if she would pray with me. I had to tell my husband I was just walking to the park with my friend. He would not let me go if I had told him the truth. Do not ask me why. Maybe he is just pure sick. My dear God, please bring some peace, joy, and understanding into my life and my children's lives.

Today I was at work. I love my job! I think the best birthday gift I could give my husband is to work. I am very grateful to have a job so I could pay for my son's swim class, food shopping, and overall anything we need. I am deeply grateful.

Today after I came home nobody was home. My daughter told me my husband's sisters had taken him and my daughter out to a Mexican restaurant which is my husband's favorite food for his birthday celebration. She told me my son did not want to go, and I need to pick him up from his friend's home. I went to Janie's home to pick up my son. She was so kind. She made me a very delicious hamburger. So I left to go home with my son, and we both thanked my friend for the great food.

My husband and daughter came home. My daughter looked sad. She hugged me and said she is sorry that they did not bring dinner for me. She wanted to, but my husband told her I do not deserve to have a nice meal. So I told her not to worry as I had dinner. He came with a food bag in his hand and handed to me. I said to him thank you, but I already ate. He said just shut up and open it. So I did. The bag was full of bones. He told me to share the bones with the dog. My daughter started to cry and left the kitchen. It was so sad. Dear God, he keeps hurting me and I just do not know what to do.

This weekend I am going to have lunch with Lorain, one of my hair clients. She called me to congratulate me for my master's degree. I cried and told her I need some legal advice. She is a very successful attorney. I am sad. I think I just cannot take this any longer. I need to get out. I need some legal advice. I am worried about money. How am I going to pay for a divorce? How about my son? I want full physical custody. Dear God, I thank you. I am praying for better days to come. Days that my husband would not feed me dog food in front of my loving children.

6/23/2007

I met my friend Lorain for lunch. She is very kind, and smart. I told her almost everything. She is an attorney and gave me some very helpful advice. According to her I could have a case. She told me if he touches me I should call the police, and since the history of the abuse is more than two decades, he may end up going to jail too. Her biggest advice was if he ever were to push or touch me or my kids, just call the police. She said the police need to have records of his poor behavior.

Then she talked about meditations and the power of our prayers. She told me she has kind of prayed for her husband to be out of her life for good. This is the prayer she gave me: "By my will, by my desire, I am asking my higher power help me to release all the negative energy in my marriage, and release them to the light. I am asking my higher power to forgive me if I have hurt anybody's feeling in the past. I am asking, by my will, by my power all my guardian angels help me to keep my husband far from me and keep him happy." She told me I should do this every day as often as I can. Then she encouraged me to start dreaming about a life without him. Where would I go, what would I do, and how free I would feel in my heart. I cried and told her the truth about how I wanted my husband to die from a heart attack or stroke. I told her I feel ashamed about my death wish for him, but his death seems to me the only path towards peace in my life. She looked at me and said this is the last time you are allowed to talk like this. According to her this was a very negative talk, and the outcome is going to be very negative. She stated I must let the higher power know what I want, but what I want must be filled with love and I need to release all this negative energy right now. Then she put some meditation music on, held my hand, and said, "Let go and let God." I felt very light. I was not anxious anymore. Her last words were, "If you talk to your higher power like this, I promise you will be free very soon." According to her, these methods guarantee successful outcomes. I was so happy after all this. I could not stop imagining a content, happy, relaxed, and prosperous life. She even wrote the prayers on a piece of paper for me. The last thing she told me while I was walking to my car was," If he ever touches your body or your children's bodies, remember there is law protecting all the abused woman and children. He has been a bad boy and he needs to learn there are consequences for his actions. You need to know you deserve love, respect, and peace." I thanked her and cried all the way home.

I was feeling mixed emotions. Part of me felt free and believed everything that Lorain told me. I felt with all my heart that my beloved God would take my husband out of my life and keep him happy. Then the other part was already processing the grief of not having a solid family for my kids. The weight of all the ongoing responsibilities of being a single parent and being the leader in my children's lives made me stop the car and just cry more. But the best part after my crying was feeling peace and being able to visualize the light on the end of tunnel. Yes, I believed with every cell in my body that my husband would be going out of my life for good in a very short time. I smiled, thanked my heavenly father, got some groceries, and made dinner for my kids. I whispered the prayers that Lorain taught me while making dinner. I went to bed and kept repeating the prayers in my head. I closed my eyes and asked God to show me more ways. I also tried to

The Breakthrough

look at my life from an outsider's point of view. It all started from conception, the miracle of my life--my father's sperm meeting my mother's egg. All the different growing pains I had to feel when I was 11 years old, and how my heart broke into so many pieces. Then there was my sister's abusive marriage, my mother's ongoing never ending depression from the moment she lost my beloved father, then my own abusive husband, my beautiful daughter's open heart surgery, ongoing financial problems, and many more sad events in my 40 years of age. I took a deep breath and put all the sad memories in an imaginary box. I wrap the box, and hand it to you my beloved God. I woke up, felt lighter, and could see life clearer.

I called a few attorneys for free consultation. My main concern was my son's full physical custody. I was told it would be very hard, almost impossible to get a full physical custody, especially if there were no criminal records, jail time, or any police report. They all said the same thing as Lorain: if he touches you call the police.

8/6/2007
8:15 AM, Santa Ana office

Dear God, I thank you for my health, my children's health, my job, and my education.

I had a very bad weekend. I have been trying to work out something for my son so while I am at work some of his friends that I trust could take him to the beach or any another fun activity. In order for me to make up for that, I would offer to babysit on weekends so the parents could have some down time. A wonderful friend I have known for the last five years asked if I could take care of her two kids on Friday night so she could go see a movie with her husband. I agreed and told her I would pick up my son and her kids at 5:30, right after I get off work. So I got my son and the kids and took them to In-and-Out Burger. Then they wanted to go swimming at the pool in our backyard.

My husband called at this time and started to cuss at me. He informed me he and his father were washing the carpets. Then he told me to buy food and carpet shampoo for him and get home right away. I got him food and the carpet shampoo and drove home. I told the kids we cannot go inside the house since the carpet is being washed. He never told me of this plan ahead of time because then I would never have offered to babysit my friend's kids at this time. But this is very typical in our marriage, no communication.

When we got home, I took the kids to the backyard and told them they cannot go inside. They were going to play, swim, and hang out in the backyard. They were having a great time. I gave my husband and his father the food. He took it from me and called me a "useless mother fucker." His poor old father was watching all this and told his son, "Do not talk to her like this. She just came home from work."

I took a deep breath, talked to my dear God, and told my husband I am sorry I did not know you were planning to wash the carpet. I will make sure the kids won't walk inside the house. He looked at me and said, "Just fuck off."

I stayed outside with all three kids, until almost 10:30 PM. Then my friend and her husband came to pick up their kids. They were in a good mood, and wanted to talk. My husband came to the backyard and saw the way I was interacting with the husband and wife. He looked angry. They were polite to him but kept ignoring him and continued talking about the movie to me. I started to feel really anxious. It was very clear to me that something bad was going to happen. Part of me wanted them to stay forever because my husband never would touch me or my kids in front of them. So listening to their conversation was like a safety blanket or shelter for me. On the other hand, I was getting very sleepy since I had been up since 6 AM, had gone to work, and had been in charge of these three kids for the last four hours.

I knew the big storm was going to happen in our house as soon as they left. My husband is from a very clean, organized family, and they do not believe in hiring anybody for help. My husband himself is lazy, hates cleaning, but likes to have a wife who works making at least $80,000 a year, is skinny, is a great cook, cleans, and takes care of the kids too. Oh, and also the wife has ongoing family parties for him and his family, because the wife's family should not be in the same city, state or make that the same continent. So by now you know, my dear God, I am not his perfect ideal wife, and when he cleans the house, he keeps reminding himself that his wife is far from perfect.

They finally left and it was late. It was warm outside, but my son was tired and cold. I helped him to get dry, and when we wanted to get in to the house he started to scream at me loudly. My husband had locked us outside and told me I have to be punished for my stupidity. I said I was sorry for not helping him with carpet cleaning, and he said, "Fuck off, you lazy whore." By this time, I started to feel so sorry for my sweet son and told my husband to open the door. He was going to make our son sick. It did not help.

Finally around 11:30pm he opened the door. My poor sweet son was almost sleeping and I was just crying hopelessly, feeling so sorry for myself. At this time all I wanted to do was to take my son upstairs, give him some dry, clean clothes, put him in his bed, kiss him good night, and then just go to sleep myself. I was very depressed, sleepy, and just done with the day. I was ready to put this day behind.

Well, I guess my mentally ill husband was just warming up for the rest of his abusive show. The minute he opened the backyard door and let us in, he started to scream and cuss at me. Then he had a water bottle in his hand that was almost full. He threw the water bottle at me, and it hit my leg very hard. I got a big bruise the next day. While he was doing all this, my poor son was right there. He said, "Mom, please call the police. He is crazy."

I was going to call, but he had already taken the home phone and my cell phone away from me. I just looked at him and told him to stop. I grabbed my son and ran upstairs. After I helped my son get ready for bed, I went to my bed myself, sat there, and started to pray more, feeling very badly. I felt with all my heart I had failed to protect my son. How sad that he is giving me the advice that I should call the police. Well, I just couldn't do it. I slept and prayed that my husband would just end the show for tonight. I was burned out emotionally and physically.

The next day was Saturday and he was gone all day. I don't know what for, but I was happy he was gone. He came home around 7:30pm and told me to get ready to go to one of his client's home for a dinner party. He was in a very good calm mood. I looked at him, started to cry, showed him my bruised leg, and told him in a very honest naive voice, "I do not want to go with you anywhere. You hit me last night. You locked our son and me out in the backyard, and you kept cussing at me and calling me names. Please divorce me peacefully. I do not have money to take you to court. Please let's just end this."

He got very angry, and told me to "get the fuck out of his life." He will take the house, my son and the two cars. After 30 minutes he came and told me if I do not go to this party with him tonight, he will not give me car keys to go to my work on Monday. I knew he was not lying and was crazy enough to do this.

I remembered how not to long ago, he took my car keys from me for no clear reason. I first begged him to give me the car keys so I could take my son to school go to work, but he didn't. I called his parents at 6:30am in the morning, and for the first time I felt brave enough to ask for help directly from his parents. I told his father would you please come to our house and talk to your son. He came right away. My husband was surprised that I had involved his older father, and he got angrier at me.

When my father-in-law walked into our home, the first thing he said to me was, "Do not bother your husband. You should know he is very emotional these days and anything could make him angry." I thanked my father-in-law for coming, and I explained the truth to him. I told him I had no idea what was going on, but I needed the car keys to go to work and take my son to school. So my father-in-law came to the family room where my husband had been sleeping for the last few years. He told my husband to stop bothering us and asked him to give the car keys to me.

My husband cussed at me in front of my son and his father. Then he told me to tell him, "I am sorry. I eat your shit." At first I was speechless. I felt numb. Then I heard my father in law's voice telling me, "Do what he says. You really hurt his feelings this time." In my head I'm thinking what is going on? Dear beloved old wise man, I asked you to come here to help me, to rescue me and my poor son, your poor smart grandson, and you are telling me to say sorry to your son? Sorry for what? Sorry for being weak? Sorry for not having my father here right now to protect me against all you monsters? Sorry for marrying your son? Sorry for my mother's stupidity to make me marry your son in three weeks? Oh dear God, the list of what I would be sorry for would go on for a long, long time.

Then I looked at the time and it was getting late. If I did not leave the house in the next eight minutes I would be late at my new work, and my son may be late for school. He cannot be late. He wanted to get the award for best attendance at the end of school year. I am under probation since I just started this job. So I took a deep breath. I talked to my beloved God in my heart. I asked him to help me to push throughout this storm right now. I asked him to be the leader and just take me somewhere far from this war zone. So I said to my husband in front of my father-in-law, and my poor son, "I am sorry. I eat your shit. Please give the car keys to me."

While I was saying these words, I heard my beloved God's voice in my heart. He said to me, "Good job. Just keep pushing through the fog. You will see the sun really soon. I will take you there. Today is not the day, but that day is just around the corner." So I knew He was capable of doing this for me.

So I took my shower, washed my tears away, and wished I could wash away the bruise in my leg and the many, many deep bruises in my heart. I got dressed, got my son ready, and went with him to this dinner party.

The next day, Sunday, my beautiful daughter was coming home from her college for summer vacation. I was so excited about seeing her! She loves my cooking and actually enjoys eating what I make for her. I started to prepare lasagna for her. When I cook I like to do few things at one time. So in one pan I was frying the meat and onions and getting the meat sauce ready. In the other pan I was boiling hot water to cook the lasagna, and I was making my salad at the kitchen table. I was so happy. My son was watching his favorite TV show. My husband was not home.

I heard the garage door open and then saw him walk into the kitchen. I started to feel uneasy in my heart. My son hid the remote control because my husband would take away the remote control anytime he felt like it without considering anybody's feeling in the room. So he walked in the kitchen and started to yell at me because I did not make his omelet. He usually plays soccer on Sundays, gets home around 11:30 to noon, and by the time he walks in I always have his omelet made, his coffee ready and the whole 9 yards. Today I was so happy my daughter was coming home, that I forgot about my husband's breakfast. He got so mad he took the boiling pan with the hot water, looked at me for few seconds, and told me he would trash my face and my body with this hot water.

In my head I started to pray hard. "Dear God, help me. Protect me, and protect my son. I do not want to have a burned body or burned face. I do not want to go to the emergency room. My daughter will be home in one hour. I do not want her to see me in the emergency room. I do not want my son to interrupt his favorite TV show by seeing his father pouring boiling hot water on his mother. Dear beloved God, help."

My husband lifted the pan and looked at my eyes with hate and disgust. Then he took the pan to the backyard and threw it all on the grass. He came back to the kitchen, took the other pan with the meat sauce, and stared at me for another few seconds. He went to backyard and threw it on the grass too.

The Breakthrough

Then he remembered the remote control for the TV. He asked my son where it was. My son got it from under the sofa, handed it to him and started to cry. He ran to his room. I ran upstairs to my son's room. I held him. He was crying and I was crying. I told him I was so sorry and I loved him.

I looked at my watch and my daughter was coming home in about 30 minutes. I had to get some food ready for her. She was looking forward to eat my cooking, although the lasagna was on the grass in the back yard. I had to pull myself together. I try to create a family for my kids. My kids need and deserve to have a home, a married mom and dad, and overall a stable home. Did I say a stable home? This home was very far from stable in many ways, but I just had to make some lunch soon. I told myself it is not the time for me to go over all the assessments in my head, how dysfunctional my life is. I thanked God that my husband did not burn me or my son with the hot water and hot meat sauce. I asked my beloved God give me courage, to push through another storm.

I started to cook and the lunch was ready in 30 minutes. My beautiful daughter looked happy to be home and was excited to eat some homemade meals. We ate together at the kitchen table like a normal family. My daughter was talking about school, and for a short period of time I forgot what had happened in that kitchen less than one hour ago. I glanced at my kids, the food, and my dog. I felt happy and grateful, until my husband opened his mouth and started making nasty comments about the food I had cooked. He changed everybody's mood. He was the master in bringing the worst out of people. So my kids and I finished our food and I thanked God for our two-story house.

We ran upstairs with some nonsense excuses. While I was helping my daughter unpack, she noticed the bruise on my leg. When she asked what that was, before I could answer, my 11 year old son told her the whole story. I felt so badly for my daughter. She got so sad, hugged me, and said she was sorry. I started to cry, and all of a sudden I heard myself saying, "I am thinking about going to the police and show them what he has done." My two kids looked at me and said nothing.

After few minutes my son told me, "It's about time, Mom. Please tell on him. He cannot treat us like this. Call the police now. I hope they take him to jail."

My daughter looked calm, and after few minutes she said, "Yah, Mom. I think you should definitely do something about this. What he has been doing is not right."

I decided to pray about this all day and all night. Monday came and I am here. I have not done anything yet, but I am really thinking about going to the police station today. Dear God, I need you to give me power and strength to make a good choice today. Dear God, I am asking for a life without my husband. Please take him far from me and my children. I am grateful to know you are listening, and you will take care of me. I know everything I want is what you desire for me, but I am tired of all this. Please remove him from my life and my children's lives. Thank you.

8/6/2007, 10:05 PM
Janie's home

Thank you, my dear God. I am grateful for my kids, my job, my health, and what I did today. I went to police station in my city. I do not know how I got there, but I did. I was very anxious. I felt guilty and ashamed at the same time. A nice older lady was sitting at the front desk. She looked at me and said I am glad you made it. We are going to be closed in few minutes. I looked at her face, and in my heart I heard a voice say, "You made it."

After few minutes a young officer, may be in his early or mid-20's, came and interviewed me. Then he asked another officer who was older to join him. They took pictures of my leg, and wrote down everything I was saying. I told them I wanted to get a divorce. They asked many questions like has he ever hit you in front of your kids, has he ever tried to kill you, and many, many more. Sadly the answers to all of them were a solid YES. I told them he is a hunter and has many guns in the home. He had tried to use his hunting knife, saying if I want a divorce he will cut my throat with that knife.

For some reason I felt safe enough to talk about rape too. I know I cannot believe I am saying the word RAPE. I admitted for the first time in my life that he had raped me many, many times. The last time was four weeks ago. He had both car keys in his pocket. When I got ready to go to work, I couldn't find the keys. I was running late. I started to look around the coffee table next to the sofa where he was sleeping. He grabbed my hand and asked me if I was going to go to fuck around at work. I said please give me the keys. I had learned in my abnormal psychology class that with people who are mentally ill, you need to talk with a calm, direct, and low voice. The sentences need to be short and you just keep repeating whatever you want with the same pattern. So I did try to use that. He got angry and asked why I was talking to him like he is crazy. You want the car keys, lie down, let me remind you who is your master, and then you can go. He started taking his clothes off, and he said your next option is to take the public bus. I just looked at him, told him he is sick, I need to go, and I do not want to touch his body or be touched by his hands. He grabbed my hair and raped me. I told the police officers he had at least raped me 25 times in the 20 years of marriage. They kept writing everything down.

After almost one and half hours they told me they need to come to my home, take his guns away, and interview my kids. I just went with the flow. As soon as I got home they followed. I felt numb. I felt like I was watching someone else's life. While I was feeling very disconnected from all of this, I saw one policeman interviewing my son, the other one was talking to my daughter, and one was sitting next to me. He asked me to show him where my husband's guns were. Oh my beloved God, I felt very present. I wanted to seize the moment when they took all his guns out of this house. I hated the idea that my husband had guns and used those guns to kill innocent animals. He kept them right next to our family room. I thanked God for this victorious moment.

While I was feeling pure joy in my heart, I saw the police officers talked together. One of them made a phone call and started to fill out a form. In about maybe 5 minutes the officer on the phone came closer to me and started to explain what a restraining order meant. He gave me the paper, read it to me, and stated the judge had decided it is not safe for you and your children to be close to your husband. I was speechless, happy, and anxious all at the same time.

They asked me where he was at this time. I told them I have no idea. He usually does not tell me where he is and when he is coming home. They told me it would be a good idea for us to be gone around the time he may be arriving home. I thanked them and told the kids let's just go to Olive Garden Restaurant.

I was not hungry at all, but we went. It was a very peaceful dinner. Nobody really talked about what had just happened. I think we were in denial. We happened to see the same friend whom I had babysat for three nights ago. I wanted to thank them for letting me to babysit, and that as a result I was breaking free from my abusive husband. I just couldn't help it. I hugged them all and felt so happy to see them.

We finished dinner, and I started to get anxious. The police called me and told me they had handed him the restraining order and he had gone. They said he was angry, but very cooperative. I told my kids we should not sleep at home. My friend Janie was so kind, and she told me we could stay at her home as long as we wanted. So here we are at her home, and for some reason I am worried what if he decides to do something to me.

Dear God I am handing you all my problems. I thank you for this moment. I thank you for the law. By my will, by my heart, by my deep desire, I am asking my heavenly father to keep my husband far from me and my kids. Keep him happy, but far away. I thank you, my dear God, for all your ongoing miracles in my life.

8/7/2007, 8:07 AM
MTP training. Santa Ana

I am so thankful to God for my health, my children's health, my master's degree, my job, my eyes, my big heart. Dear God, thank you for the gift of life. Dear God, I have no regret about what I did yesterday. I feel free.

8/8/07, 9:50 AM
Office

I am sitting in this training and my mind is everywhere. I want to extend my restraining order to three years. I do not trust him. His family has called me and asked me to stop all this and go for a peaceful separation. I told them I do not trust him. I want him out of my life, my heart, and as far as he could go. I am going to do whatever I can to get full custody of my son. I will not let him hurt my son anymore. I am worried about money, attorney fees, and my daughter's college tuition. I am meeting one of my best friends, Karen, for lunch (my client when I was a hair dresser, my mentor, and my spiritual mother). I am going to see if I could borrow some money from her for attorney consultation fees. I am praying for favors, dear God.

8/9/07
Home

Dear God, I met with Karen yesterday. She gave me a check for $2500 and told me to use it wisely to hire an attorney. I am deeply grateful. I thanked her, I cried, and couldn't really eat lunch. I just cried, told her I was burned out, and had nothing left to fight in this marriage. I hugged her and told her right now she was my guardian angel because I did not have the money to go ahead with my divorce plans. After that I just called a few attorneys. All of them told me that if I want to get my son's full custody and overall have more peace, I should extend the restraining order from three days to 25 days.

Dear God, on one hand I am so happy, and on other hand I am feeling sorry for myself and my kids that we have to go through this. The word restraining order sounds very powerful and dysfunctional at the same time.

So I went to court by myself. I filled out the same forms I helped my clients fill out in the shelter four years ago. I prayed that my dear God would be holding me together and He did. I wrote a few pages when I was asked to explain any past physical abuse, sexual assault, and emotional abuse. I felt I wanted to make a deep personal connection with the judge who was reading my request. I did not hold anything back. I just vented like I do when writing in my journal or sharing my pain with you, my beloved God. I cried while I was writing. I needed more pages; one page was not enough to share my 20 years of ongoing pain. So I used more pages. I just let go and let God.

As soon as I turned in my request I prayed more. I prayed that I would be done seeing him for a while or forever. At this time I had some moments of joy. I remembered my beautiful cousins who were cleaning the kitchen with me the day we got the phone call about my father.

One of my cousins, Marjan, had eyes that changed color depending on what she wore. Her eye color changed from green to blue, and sometimes hazel. Marjan was engaged when she was 11 years old to a man who was 14 years older than she was. She got married to him when she was 15. It was an arranged marriage by her parents, as they believed she was too beautiful and if she did not get married she may get raped. I'll never forget her wedding day. She looked like a doll. She was too perfect to be real. She had no idea how this day was the beginning of a very dark chapter in her life for many years. Her husband turned out to be a sick abusive man who was very insecure. She got divorced 35 years later. She cried and cried for years. She asked and begged for a divorce. Finally she got it because he decided he didn't want her anymore. She had no power over her life, her marriage, and her divorce. Today she is divorced, but has no hope to remarry again, and is still trying to recover from all the pain she had gone through.

Her beautiful spirit is still healing from all the wounds. God knows when and how she can ever recover. Maybe if she had divorced him earlier she would have had more energy to reestablish herself. All I know is that I am grateful to be here right now.

I am thinking about my other cousin who got killed one year after my father's death, Mina. She was Marjan's younger sister. Mina also had beautiful eyes. They were the perfect shade of turquoise. Her skin color was dark tan. This contrast of her eyes and skin was purely God's art. Then her personality made her more outstanding. She was vibrant, fun, and smart. Her parents arranged her marriage to a distant family member when she was only 15 years old. There was nothing wrong with the guy. He had a job, was educated, and he wanted to marry this beautiful teenager. Although she was not ready, she was forced to get married and she started loving him afterwards. She got killed while she was walking with her husband in the streets of Tehran during the Iranian Revolution. I am thinking about her and what her life could have been like if she hadn't died so young and how her marriage would be.

I am also thinking about my beautiful talented sister, who finally got her divorce after 17 years of ongoing daily physical and emotional abuse. It was like a miracle when her husband finally agreed to sign the divorce papers. She is now working full-time as a very successful designer in my country. I am thinking about her beautiful face. I am wondering if my father were alive, would he agree to let my smart, talented sister get married at 17, or would he disagree to arrange these awful teenage marriages for my sister and me? I know he would not. I just know he valued education, and he would never agree on arranged marriages for his daughters at that age. I miss my father so much right now.

My name was called. Thank you, God. I was approved. I did not have to explain my case face-to-face with the judge. It was just signed and I got 25 days of freedom from my husband. I came home, called my friends, and told my children as well. My son got very happy, but my daughter looked sad.

My sister called and stated she will be coming to help and support me in the next tow to three weeks. God, thank you. Today was a very long, but empowering day. For the first time in a long time, I am deeply grateful for all the pain you are putting me through. I know you are trying to shape me to become an independent courageous woman, not a pretty face with a small brain. Not the peanut size brain my husband would have me believe. I know today my brain is a normal size. Thank you, God, for showing me that I don't need to be afraid of him anymore. I am releasing all the negative energy to you, my dear heavenly father. I am ready to put a closure to this chapter and am deeply excited for the new chapter.

My dear son looked sad today. Dear God, please bring some sparkle back to his beautiful eyes. I am open to receive whatever you want to give me. So far everything is just too good to be true. My husband is out of the house. I closed my eyes and remembered how many times he had locked me and our loving son outside of the house. Well today, thanks to the law, he is not only locked out of the house, he is not supposed to be on our street or anywhere close to me and to my children. Thank you, my dear father, for this freedom. It is priceless.

8/15/2007

Dear God thank you for everything. My sister came from Iran to see if she could help me. She is very loving, and I feel so blessed that she is here for me and my kids. They need some support.

Dear God, my son looks very sad. He cried last night and I tried to talk to him. He told me he will talk when he is ready. I am praying for healing of his broken heart. I lost my father when I was 11 years old, and what a sad coincidence my poor son is feeling a lost in his heart too. I hope, my dear God, what I did would help my son to have more peace in his life. I am ready, my Lord, to do whatever you want me to do in order to protect, promote, and provide for my children.

8/19/2007

For the first time I realized I am very poor, because my beautiful sister traveled few thousand miles to come visit me and my kids, and I have to work. I am so sad, because every cell of my body wants to be next to her, talking, drinking tea, and just spending time with her. Since I just started my job two months ago I have no vacation time. I am living paycheck to paycheck and I need this job badly. I cried all the way to work. I felt sorry for my kids, myself, and my poor sister. She has her own housekeeper, hates cleaning and cooking, but since she got here she has been taking over all the house responsibilities. I am deeply grateful for having her in my life, and it breaks my heart any time I realize I do not live close to her or any member of my family. I learned in one of my classes that usually abusive partners would isolate their partner from their family and friends. He sure did isolate me and I guess it worked for him. My sister gave me some money for my attorney's fees. I am speechless for her love and support. I am grateful for my education, my job, and because of them I was able to leave my husband. So dear God, please forgive me.

8/23/2007

Dear God, my sister suggested there should be a meeting between my husband, my sister, and three of her close friends so they could talk about the divorce process to my husband. The goal would be to find a way to make this divorce quickly, without spending too much money on attorneys' fees. This kind of meeting is very common in my culture. There is this traditional belief that family and friends could intervene and save the marriage, or overall help the couple that is in crisis. Although I did not see any need to do this, I respected my sister and agreed. I couldn't be in that meeting due to beloved restraining order.

Yesterday I got a call from the district attorney's office, stating my husband's case is being considered a criminal case and he is going to go on trial 10/30/07. When I asked why, he explained calmly, "After reviewing the whole report we believe he needs to be prosecuted for domestic violence and battery. We believe there had been a long history of abuse and sexual assault, and he needs to come to court defend his case and his reasons for doing what he did." I asked what would be some common outcomes for something like this. He answered, "It depends. He may go to jail for 6 months to 3 years, and this is probably is the worst outcome for him. If he pled guilty he may just get some community service hours, anger management classes, parenting classes, and criminal restraining order from you and your son if you get the full physical custody." I asked if there was anything I could do to make this go away for him because I feel so badly for my husband. He answered, "There is nothing you can do. The police receive many, many domestic violence calls. Only very few of them have the judge issue the restraining order after two hours of receiving the report. Only one to maybe four cases get chosen by the DA, due to the severity of the abuse that the DA believes has gone on for years. Your case was just a very special case. We just could not ignore it. Although the report says he threw the bottle of water at you, you got some bruise on your leg, and you went to police station three days after, we know there is more. Even if you have changed your mind and forgiven him for what he had done, the law has not. We want to make sure he gets some punishment for what he had done."

I was just crying. Tears were coming down like Niagara Falls. If my tears had a voice these are the words they would say, "Wow! My dear beloved God, what have you done? I am deeply grateful. Thanks to you dear district attorney, thanks to you God, and thanks to your mother for giving birth to you. Thanks for your amazing brain. Thank you for being able to feel my 21 years of ongoing struggles. Thanks for trying to punish the spoiled, out- of-control monster who was a mentally, physically, and financially abusive man that I shared 21 years of my life with. Thank you for caring."

I took a deep breath and told the DA thanks for his time. He asked if he could call me in the next few weeks. I said definitely. He said, "Just to let you know, you are not paying me to help you. The state is paying me to protect you. The case is out of your hands too. Even if he moves in with you tomorrow, we will still go ahead with our plans." I told him there is a restraining order against him, I still do not feel safe, and thanked him again.

Going back to the meeting, last night my sister and her friends informed my husband about the phone call from the DA. I guess he got very sad. He had told everybody he loves his son. Overall he loves his family and doesn't want to lose them, but if this is what I want he will respect that. He had three requests: that I should cancel the restraining order, agree to full joint physical and legal custody, and move out of the house so he could sell it. My sister said he looked very disturbed and was not very talkative. I really felt sorry for him, and I prayed he would be open to listening. I was wrong. He left and told them he was not going to stop fighting to get his son. I am praying for a peaceful ending.

8/30/2001, 9:10 AM
COURTROOM L63

Dear God, dear Lord of the universe, I am sitting in the courtroom, waiting. I need you my dear Father, to stay with me all the way. I am calling on all my guardian angels to come and help me. My intentions are to keep my husband as far away from my children and me as possible. I want to extend the restraining order. I have faith in my amazing attorney. I consulted a few attorneys but I liked this one because he is peaceful and I believe he knows what he is doing. We are similar. We're both driven, goal oriented, courageous, and very creative, too. Overall I felt good about his energy.

I am sitting here and I am feeling anxious. The court is small; only about 20 people are here. I am sitting next to my attorney and I see all of my husband's family on the opposite side. It is so sad to see all the people I used to see at Christmas parties, Iranian New Year celebrations, and at the countless dinner and lunch parties. They were there for the birth of my children and I was there for the birth of their children. There are just too many good memories. I really honestly cannot think of any bad memories with them. They have been very kind to me and my children. I am thinking about the time I married my husband at 19 and moved away from my family. I started to like his family right away. I wanted to fill up my empty heart with their love and started to believe they really liked me, too, and wanted them to be part of my life forever. It saddens me that they do not even want to look at me now. They look at me like I have committed some crime. Although on many occasions they had showed their sympathy towards me, today they are looking at me with pure hatred. I can see it and I can feel it. I remember when I first came to the United States. After spending a few days with my sister-in-law, who is only two years older than I am, she told me that if I were her friend she would never let me marry her brother. I looked at her and wondered why or how she could say something like that. I actually just asked her, "Why not?" Her answer was just to wait and I would see why. Now, I am here sad and worried because the weight of their anger towards me is heavy.

Three nights ago my husband's brother-in-law came to talk to me. One of them is a middle-aged Iranian man who seemed like a very caring man, someone who cared deeply for his family. Mostly, he has been polite and respectful toward my kids and me. He came and after talking for a while he told me I should try to give my husband another chance. I thanked him, told him my mind was made up, and he was very understanding. He assured me he would always respect me as his sister-in-law regardless of the outcome and instructed me to let him know if there was anything he could do for me to help my children and me. His last words were, "Please remember you have a brother who lives 10 minutes away from you. Please give me a call if you ever need any help with anything. I am here to help and I am sorry about your divorce. Please call me and let me know if there is anything I can do for you or your children."

My other brother-in-law, who is Caucasian, is also a very kind and caring man. He came to my house and talked about his own personal experience with domestic violence when he was a child. He expressed his concerns, not for my safety of the safety of my children, but for his wife. He stated, "I am sorry for what you have to go through, but what you are doing to your husband is affecting my wife. She cries every night because she is worried about her brother and I cannot stand to see my wife crying. This really is killing me and I feel hopeless. I want her stop crying."

As I was listening to him, I asked to God to control my mouth. The real person inside me wanted to say, "How dare you! How could you come to my house, in my kitchen, with the intention of helping us when the real reason you are here is to convince me to remove the restraining order and jeopardize my safety and my children's safety? How could you want me to go back to a man who has no heart, soul, or sense of compassion, who had abused me and my children so many, many times, just because you are sad when your wife cries? How selfish you can you be?" Thank God my prayers worked and I just looked at him and complimented him on his love for his wife. I thanked him for stopping by and I told him I would go through with the divorce, that I would not remove the restraining order, and that there was no way things could go back to the way they were. He got up, said he is sorry for all this, and started to walk out. I was right behind him. He stopped, looked in my eyes, and said, "If I see you or your children I will not talk to any of you. I guess this is the end of our family connection. I need to respect my wife and her family. I am so sorry but I know you understand." He then left.

I was speechless and after few minutes I was weeping and praying at the same time. It was then that I decided that if having peace in my life meant not having my in-laws in my life, it would be worth it. I just prayed they would change their narrow, judgmental minds. I hoped they would remain in my children's lives. Then I prayed and asked God to be the love, rock, and everything for my children and me. I remembered that my kids would always have my family in Iran who would always love them.

When my brothers-in-law saw me today, both completely ignored me. They walked next to their wives and did not even make eye contact with me. I am praying to my beloved God to help me. I need you, dear

God. Please help all of us to release all the negative energy and grasp at the light. I have you in my heart. I am not alone. I love you and I know you will take care of me all the way, not just halfway. Thank you, Lord. I wish I had my family in this county. They keep calling me all the time but today it would be nice to hold them and feel the human connection in this cold court room. Dear God, do not let me throw a pity party for myself. I need to stop right now. I feel all my guardian angels with me at this time.

My attorney just informed me the next hearing would be in two months, the restraining order is in effect, and we will be going for child custody investigations in six weeks. I am grateful, dear God. Thank you.

In the next few weeks I had days where I felt very overwhelmed, tired, and fearful about all the things that were happening at the same time. I see ten unpaid bills in my mailbox. Some have next-day payment deadlines and others are late notices as my husband had stopped paying the monthly bills including my daughter's college tuition. Fortunately, my friend, Janie, and her mother gave me a check which I mailed express delivery. At least I could take care of that for my daughter -- I wonder how much pain I have caused with the thought that I have taken her father away from her. Oh God, it is so difficult looking at her sad beautiful eyes. The whole ordeal seems easier for my son. I have found a great therapist who has a lot of experience with children. I took my son to see him a few times. He was expensive but I wanted to have the best person. After seeing my son a few times, he told me not to worry about him. He was loving school, had big dreams and goals, loved me, and he had stored his father in a box with all bad memories. He was not ready to open it. I asked the therapist if it was normal for my son not to want to deal with it or to talk about his father. The therapist assured me, "Your son is doing great. In times of great crises, it is normal for children and adults to try to put it behind them to move forward. Your son genuinely loves you and knows you are very strong and protective. He will be fine and keep doing what ever you are doing because it is working." I asked him if I should encourage my son to be involved with his father to which he said that my son was a very smart 11-year-old. I was to respect his wishes. My son had told me he had no desire to see his father and in his heart his father died when he was four years old. I thanked the therapist and left so I would not hold him up from his other clients. When I asked him if we should come back in two or three weeks, he said, "My work with your son is done. There is nothing I could do to help him. He is doing great but call me if you feel like it is an emergency. However, my job is done. Your son is just fine." On my way home I wept and thanked God.

My daughter was doing well, too, though I was worried. My attorney told me it would be a good idea to include any witnesses to domestic violence like my mother, family member or friend. I called my mother and she came one week before my court date. She was very sad, weak, and anxious. I tried to see if I could rely on her, and at the end I decided she was too weak and emotional to endure the trial. My mother is one of the kindest people on earth and I worried that if she saw my husband in the court she would become emotional and cry.

I decided not to tell anyone at work, aside from three close friends, about my divorce. I did not want or need anyone's pity. I have days when I cry alone and sometimes I think I am processing the grief I feel for leaving my family behind, all the family love and connections that I had missed, a stable and loving marriage which I did not have. I was merely at home with my children and nothing else going in my life. I had no work, no school, no internship, nothing. I only wanted to be a full-time mother without a million other things going on in my life at the same time. There are days I look at their eyes and I just want to beg them for forgiveness for not being able to provide them a normal, peaceful, stable family life.

10/21/07

Dear God, my mother is here and I have so much anger towards her. I cannot control myself. She is the person who did this to me and although she completely denies this, it was she who forced me to marry my husband. I was a 19-year-old girl with no intention of getting married but it was she who arranged the whole event in her passive aggressive manner. She nearly fainted when I told her I had no wish to marry at this age and that I had no desire to marry this man. She told me she would never attend a wedding ceremony for me to any other man and that I would never have her blessings. While my mother will deny this completely, I have my sister as a witness; my brother was too young to remember any of this. I love my mother but it is difficult for me to sit and have a conversation with her. The worst part is the Iranian culture which values hospitality. You must respect your guests all the time. I am trying very hard to practice what I preach now as a marriage and family therapist. Compassion is the key to any broken heart; it opens all doors. I am praying that my beloved God will bless me with extra compassion towards my poor mother. Dear God please help me to forgive her; forget how she forced me to marry this crazy, manipulative, abusive stranger in three weeks, and move on in my relationship with her. Dear God I am praying you replace all my resentment towards her with love and compassion. I did have a long sad talk with her. I cried and she cried. She still did not admit that she forced me to marry. She said, "As a single mother I did my best under the circumstances I was in. You were too beautiful I was afraid you would fall in love with some loser and become pregnant. So I married you to this educated, calm, nice looking man and it seemed such a safe marriage to me. I am so sorry for all the pain you had to endure and that you endure now." There are days when I come home and I am glad she is here to take care of my son, to be with him, talk with him, and to feed him. For that I am deeply grateful. I want to hold her and thank her for all of her unconditional love, for flying several thousands of miles to be with me and my kids through this storm, and for taking care of my home during this. But for some sad reason, the anger in me is too strong. I have built this wall between us. I cannot hug or kiss her, which is the norm in Iranian culture. Though I do force myself to give her a hug once in awhile, I am ashamed about this inability to express my love. Oh dear God this is so wrong. I hate myself for feeling this way. I know you will help me. Today the minute I came home I just gave her a hug, told her I have a headache, and went to my room. I took a long bubble bath and I prayed that you would help me. My poor mother has been home alone all by herself all day. I left this morning with my son around 7:30am and we came home at around 5 o'clock. She has been looking forward to see me, and I do love her but I just want to be by myself in my bedroom, thinking about my court hearings, my kids, work, and think out how I will survive all these upcoming storms. My attorney and friends have told me not to take my mother to the courthouse because she may not be able to control her emotions. I am sad about this, too. Dear beloved God please help me to be kind to my mother and bring down this wall I have created. I am praying to hear positive feedback from the child custody investigation report. The judge had assigned another therapist to interview all of us separately. I told her the truth and I did not ask my son to reveal to me all the things he had told her. All he said to me was, "I hope she is smart and that she gets the fact that my father was very mean to me and that I do not want to see his face or be around him." Last week a social worker went to my son's school to interview him about what his father had done to him. Oh my dear God. I was both anxious and angry at what my son's day had become. I kept telling myself that my poor son had to be pulled out of the classroom to talk about what his father did and did not do to him. I felt weak and hopeless. I hated myself for staying too long in this marriage. I wished I had left my husband in November of 1998, after he hit me so hard that I had huge bruises all over my body for over a week. If I had left my husband then, my boy would have been two years old. He would not be able to explain how and what his father had done to him and his mother. Dear God why did I do this to myself and to my beautiful children. A good mother's job is to protect, provide, and promote for her children. I am too late. I waited so long to get out of this. Oh my dear God please help me to stop right now. I just was not ready in 1998 and I did not have the backbone; my deep relationship with you was not there in those days. I did not have any education and my job was not secure. Dear God I am not going to cry over spilled milk. I know it took me a long time to clean the mess that was a created. Please forgive me for staying. I am praying my kids and their children, my beautiful grandchildren, will forgive me for staying too long. I am praying my son never remembers the social worker interview at his school. I pray the outcome of the interview will be worth the emotional pain my son has gone through. I pray for forgiveness in his heart. I pray for extra blessings and I pray you keep my husband far from me and my children. I pray for a great report from the court therapist. Thank you my dear God.

10/24/07

My dear Father, the court therapist report came. Thank you. She recommends full physical and legal custody to the mother and supervised visitation with the father based on the opinions of my son, the father, and me. She phoned to talk briefly with my daughter. Dear God, thank you. My attorney told me this will help us immensely in the final custody decisions. This is what I am praying. Dear God, I promised my son I would fight for him and protect him. Please help me to keep my promises.

Thank you dear father.

10/29/07

I did not go to court on Friday. My husband's attorney requested to postpone the court date to November 30th, to which we agreed. His attorney requested a meeting with my attorney at the courthouse so my attorney went. We agreed that if my husband was there it would be a good chance for my attorney to serve my husband the divorce papers. He did. When he served him the divorce papers my husband, enraged, threw the papers down. His attorney was embarrassed. My attorney told me that in the fifteen years of practicing law he had never seen such a childish tantrum in the courtroom. I was so happy that I was not there. My husband was given permission to come to the garage to get his clothes, files, and his computer. Thank you my dear God. The same wonderful police officer who came to my home to interview my kids came Saturday morning. He walked me to my car and I gave him the garage opener. Meanwhile, my husband and his sisters were out front waiting for me to leave and also to receive permission from the police officer to gather his things from the garage. His allotted time to execute this was 8:30 am until 12:30 pm. Thank you God for all your protection. The night before I decided to get my mother out of the house for her protection; she is very loving and emotional. The sight of my husband and his family would be too much for her to emotionally handle. I also worried that my husband might record and use in court whatever my mother might have said. After all, he was the type of man to do this and he was capable. While I was going through his belongings, I found five tapes that were voice recordings of all my conversations on the phone with my family on the phone. He had dated them and written down the names of the people involved. This is so sick. I was very angry when I found the tapes.

I just found out he has another son in England. I found seven letters addressed to my husband and dated from April until August of 1986. They are all written by a pregnant young woman begging my husband to come back to her and her unborn baby. I cried all night after I finished one of the letters.

In the letters, she writes, "My dear handsome boyfriend, my loving baby's father, why are you ignoring my letters? I am having your baby. We are going to become parents. I miss you like crazy. I talk to our baby every day and tell him stories about how handsome and kind his father is. I wish you were here with us. I really need you emotionally and also financially. My father is very sad about my pregnancy and has kicked me out. I have gone to social services. They are going to help me find housing. They have also told me if you do not come when the baby is born they will pay for all his basic needs since I am too young to work and go to school. They are encouraging me to consider school or learn some skills so that, eventually, I can support myself and the baby if you decide to not be a part of our lives.

Thinking about all this saddens me. I am crying. I cannot imagine my life without you. I love you so much. I miss you like crazy. I know when I first told you I was pregnant you became angry and questioned how I could be so sure you were its father. Do you remember our conversation? I told you I was a virgin when we met and you loved that. I told you were the first and only person with whom I had ever had sex. How could you forget our first night that we slept together? It was the best night of my life. You told me that it was the best night of your life, too. Have you forgotten how my father was? He was so hard on me and I had to lie to him anytime I wanted to see you. Please believe me. This is the time I need you, more than ever. I have lost my father's love and support. I miss my mother every day and this pregnancy has made me more emotional than usual. I want her so badly and I really need her. I am always saddened by the fact that her death means I cannot have her near during my hour of need. I know she would have protected me against my father's harsh punishments. She would not let him kick me out, with or without a baby. Oh I am so sorry for nagging so much. All I need is you and my baby. We will make our own family. Please call me or write to me. Wouldn't it be so amazing if you would just come one day and, really soon, surprise me and our baby? Please do not make fun of me if I am too fat. Remember I am eating for two. I hope the baby is a boy and I want him to be a copy of you. I love you. I miss you. Please, please call, or write to me soon. The baby is due in 4 months."

Dear God how could he do that to that poor pregnant young girl? In the next few letters that I read it was all the same sad story. She kept telling him how much she loved him and how she is hoping for a day that he would surprise her. I cried more when I felt how hopeful she was. When we got married in June of 1986, he was very quiet and distant from his surroundings. He was not a joyful, happy groom. Although I was 19 years old and very naive I reassured my sister that this was normal. She reassured me that some grooms were shy and suggested that he, too, was one of those shy grooms. Little did either of us know that he had impregnated a girl while he was working in England just two months before my marriage.

After reading all of those letters, I saw one with a photo of a beautiful baby boy. It was a photo dated ten days after our wedding and the baby photo could have just as easily been a baby photo of one of our children. If I put my children's baby pictures alongside that beautiful baby picture, no one could guess which one is which. The similarity among the three of them was so strong that they could look like full siblings. My two children do not look like me at all; they look like their father and his family. This beautiful baby, too, looked like his father who never gave him a chance to get to know him. Maybe though this baby was lucky that he didn't live through what my children did. It is all just too sad.

After reading the letters, I hated my husband even more. I felt disgusted at myself for being his wife for 21 years. How could he keep this from me? I would have loved to meet his son and to help his son in any way that I could. My kids would have loved to have an older half-brother. On the other hand, what kind of human being would impregnate a young virgin girl in then abandon her? He then has the nerve to go to Iran, find a young virgin girl who has lost her father eight years prior, marry her, make her pregnant, and keep her away from her family and friends.

I started to pack his stuff, everything that reminded me of him. I thank you, my Father, for taking this sick man out of my life and my children's lives. I hate him with every cell in my body. Yet what he did to her, we now do to him; he dumped the young girl and her newborn son, who loved him so much, and today my son and I are dumping him. Thank you, Father.

My mother is very depressed and bored. She was invited to her friend's home in Los Angeles and I decided to take her. It took me four hours to fight through the heavy Friday traffic, but I felt bad for her and for myself. She looked very sad and she needed to socialize and I needed to spend some time alone with my son and my daughter. My sister called and told me all of our friends and family in Iran are praying for me. I have a lot in my head about my husband's son in England and how he kept this from me. I am worried about the outcome of my divorce. I am going to stay positive.

The next few days were normal days filled with typical daily struggles as a newly-separated woman who has been emotionally separated from her husband for 10 years. It is busy but I am managing. My therapist has been such an amazing gift from God. She has some special training in dream analysis. I had such a strange dream last night. I told my dream to Sue, my therapist, and she analyzed it.

In my dream, our house was on fire and I was in it. Smoke was escaping from every room but noticeably from the master bedroom which was our bedroom. My son was happy, swimming in the pool. All of the five bedrooms were burning, one by one. I was trying to put the fire out one room at a time but was armed with just water bottles. All the neighbors came and asked me if they should call for help but I kept refusing, trying to convince them that I had it under control. I would try to put out the fire with my water bottle one room at a time. I extinguished the fire in one room and started on another but by that time, the fire in the first room would return. I felt out of control and frightened but I would not give up. When my husband returned home in my dream, he was enraged by the sight of the smoke and fire. "What the fuck have you done to the house, you shit head bitch?" he shouted. I responded, "I am sorry. Stop screaming. There are people here and there is a therapist in the other room and she wants to talk to you." In the room he was met by an older woman sitting behind a desk. She closed the door, talked to him and when he came out of the room he seemed very calm. I went inside to ask the therapist what she had told him. She stated she just told him what he wanted to hear, "Yes, the fire was all your wife's fault." This angered me. "I did not set the fire! Why did you lie to him?" I yelled. She said that it was the only way he would stop yelling.

After explaining the dream to Sue, she analyzed it. The fire was the rage and anger I was feeling. She believed the therapist was the wise, mature part of me which had always known the truth. However, my husband's abusiveness had made me too afraid to express the truth to him.

I remembered feeling the need to lie to him all the time. I would lie even about the stupidest things. Last year one of my friends invited my children and me out to celebrate my birthday a few weeks after my actual birthday. She had her two children and I had mine. I knew if I had told him the truth he would have taken away the car keys and prohibited me from going. So I lied to him and told him that we were going to Target to buy some new cooking pans. After the dinner, I had to rush to Target to purchase the cooking pans then returned home with my children. The fire and the smoke represented the ongoing fights in our home, especially within the bedroom, where most of our fights took place. The attempt to extinguish the fire on my own and armed only with small water bottles showed my strength and courage. Yet, at the same time, it also represented my denial regarding the actual severity of our marital conflicts. By refusing help from the neighbors or from emergency rescue, I was attempting to hide my shame from everyone. Finally, my son swimming in the pool, despite the surrounding smoke and fire all around, represented his happiness and ability to release the problem.

Around Thanksgiving Day, I was feeling sad for my daughter. We used to have big family gatherings with my husband's family. I knew in my heart my daughter was missing all that so I tried to make plans for dinner. We went to my best friend's home for lunch. She had been divorced for two years and had two daughters. It was a small and fun gathering. We all were having fun but I had made a mistake to make arrangements to go to another big Thanksgiving party to another dear friend's home. The minute we got there I felt like an outsider. My daughter looked extremely uncomfortable and even my mother, who loves all these big social gatherings, looked lost and out of place. We left after just 45 minutes. I came home and apologized to my kids and my mother. I cried and told them I am not used to being the leader of the family. "Please try to understand. I am so sorry for making you all feel so uncomfortable." I then walked to my room, closed the door, cried for a long while, came out and watched some movies with my family. I guess this day was confirming to me that I was going to be divorced. I needed to get used to not having huge fun gatherings with families since I no longer had my in-laws and my family lived oceans away.

I met with my attorney a few days after Thanksgiving and, for no reason, I started to cry. He said it was very normal and that I was grieving the loss of the family unit. Even if the unit was not perfect, it was a unit and it would take some time to get used to all the new changes. I thanked him for normalizing the situation for me and asked him to pray for me.

I left the meeting early and met with my therapist. I just love her so much. She told me the unit that I was talking and thinking about was just an illusion. She reminded me how I had always felt lonely and isolated in all my husband's family parties. I was reminded of when I had to take care of my newborns, it was just us, me and my babies. She reminded me of how I cried for days after the birth of my two children, since I had none of my family here to help me take care of myself and the baby. My in-laws had the best intentions to help me and to be there for me but I felt so lonely, sad, isolated and hopeless. Since my husband's family, when gathered, would speak in Azeri, a language I did not understand, my feelings of isolation would heighten. When we had dinner parties in our home soon after the birth of my children, I was still in much so much pain that I could not sit, sleep, talk, or eat. It was so overwhelming that I felt suffocated. My husband would stay with them, entertain them and I just hated all that loud noise. I felt sorry for myself and my babies. It was thanks to my therapist that I was able to remember how miserable I actually was during those family gatherings. She suggested that my children and I start our own holiday traditions which was an idea I absolutely loved. I decided for next Thanksgiving and Christmas, we would go somewhere. I did not know where to go but it would be at least out of Orange County.

1/25/08, 9:15 AM
In the courtroom

Dear God, I am sitting in this court room. I see my husband, his sweet old father, and his cousin. His friend has just walked up, too. They all look sad and are doing their best to ignore me. I am keeping it together with you and my amazingly strong attorney. It is sad to see my father-in-law is sitting so close to me but he hates me. I feel the tension. I wish none of us had to be here today. I wish my abusive husband would have granted me my divorce peacefully. I wish he had moved to another country, fallen in love, and started a new family. Oh, I wish he would respect my request for him to get out of my life permanently. I gave him 21 years of my life beginning as a 19-year-old virgin, who loved him, praised him, tried so hard to be the woman he wanted me to become. He wanted an educated wife. I became that. He wanted to have family gatherings -- composed of his own family, as mine was living thousands of miles away. I gave that to him; I gave birth to two amazing children, a boy and a girl. Oh, my God, the list just goes on and on. Everyday, I cooked for him and oh, how he loved to eat. I always had tea prepared for him seven days a week, careful to be mindful of the time. If the tea I made at 8 o'clock in the evening was still waiting for his return from work at 9 o'clock, as was frequently the case, I would prepare another pot. I always meticulously cooked side dishes too like salads, fresh herbs, and yogurt dip. I admit, I was not one of those very clean, organized housewives -- I hated cleaning and organizing -- but I did the basic cleaning while I was working full-time and went to school full time, did the grocery shopping, helped at my son's classroom once a week as a room-mom, and went to all of my daughter's cross country races and all her track meets. I wanted him to notice but what he did, instead, was to convince me that I was not good enough in all of the areas in which I tried to succeed. He made sure to burst my balloon any time he felt he could. He made sure to make me understand that any thoughts or opinions I had bore no significance and were not of any importance to anyone. Dear God, I am tired of crying. I am exhausted from constantly questioning if I mattered. I am tired of asking, "Am I a loser? Am I a bad housewife? Am I a stupid mother who has no idea how to raise my kids? Am I just a hopeless slave to this man?" No, my dear God. I am your child and therefore, I matter. I am so happy to be sitting here in this room right now. I am speechless for all the peace and power you have provided me. Dear God, I know he is sorry. I know he is hurting but I have no regrets on getting him out of my life. The restraining order was my only way out and if the restraining order made my dear father-in-law sad or my mother-in-law angry, I am so sorry. I wish I could get him out of my family but still keep his family in my children's lives but they are very angry at me. To punish me his family is pulling away from my children, too. Dear God, I am praying you bless his parents with peace and acceptance and I pray they forgive me for what I did to their son but I needed to do this to protect my son. I do not want my son to assume it normal to constantly call your wife "bitch," check her cell phone, read her emails, record her conversations on the phone, read her personal journal, to attack her verbally, abuse her, and beat her. Dear God, I know it is kind of late for my daughter -- she is 20 years old now -- and she had to witness so much but I am staying positive. I hope she will learn from my divorce and the restraining order that as a woman in this amazing country, she has power to ask for help from the law to stop the cycle of the violence. Today, I am sitting here defending my rights and my children's rights. I have made many -- so many -- mistakes by letting the spoiled brat of a husband, who has never been disciplined in his life, walk all over me, crush my soul and my spirit, and smash my ego over and over. However, dear God, I am here to say to him that I may be broken but I will heal and you, my dear God, are the leader of my life. I am not alone anymore. You are going to walk me through the storm.

10:36 AM
THE COURTHOUSE COFFEE SHOP

I had only been waiting here for a few minutes when my attorney came to tell me the judge had approved the recommendation from the court therapist. The order states that my son is to live with me full-time with one supervised visit, per week, from his father. Also, the restraining order is to remain active until my husband's criminal case is resolved. My attorney also has informed me that he had contacted the DA's office and was told my husband has postponed his court hearing. I feel good about all of these. All I am thinking is that this crazy man needs to be contained, away from me, and away from my beautiful children. I am also told that my husband had finished his six months of anger management, domestic violence batterer's treatment, and parenting classes. He has another six months to go. He has earned a perfect attendance certificate but do I care? Do I think all the training in the world will change him? Do I believe in my heart he is remorseful for all he has done to me and my kids? I would hate to say "no" to all these questions. I begged him for five years to seek professional help and I was only met by his response, "Fuck you." For the last 21 years I had begged him to stop verbally abusing our children and to show them some love. All he had to say was, "Who the hell are you to teach me how to talk to my kids? Fuck you." My dear beloved God, I thank you for intervening. I thank you for justice. I thank you for today. I am going to leave now to spend some time with my son.

10:00 PM THAT SAME DAY
MY BEDROOM

Dear God, while I was getting ready to leave the courthouse coffee shop with my attorney, my husband's attorney walked toward me to show me my husband's perfect attendance certificates he had earned in his classes. With those, she added, "You need to take it easy and be friends with your husband. He is not your enemy; he is the father of your children." She continued on and on, mentioned that she, too, was divorced but still had a great relationship with her ex-husband in order to work, as a team, to raise their two children. She suggested the same for us. Though I listened politely, I tried hard to ignore the stench of her mouth which seemed to be infused with raw onion, cigarettes, and the nonsense she was spewing. I held my tongue and prayed, "Dear God, I ask you to control my mouth. I have never been so tempted to use every curse word I have ever learned. Instead, I thank you deeply for changing of my heart and my mouth."

I looked at her with compassion and respect. Actually, I admired her strength for being a full-time working single mother. I praised her for wanting to help damaged people like my husband. I started to look at her like I would my sister. She was not my enemy; she was a sister. We are all God's children. I shook her hand, looked into her eyes, and said, "Thank you for trying to help us with our divorce. God bless you. I know there is a lot going on. Thank you for taking your time showing me my husband's certificates. I pray that the classes were helpful for my husband. I pray he will change for himself and his kids and I am very happy for you and your ex-husband and your great relationship. I do agree that kids need to be in touch with both parents regardless of divorce or any major changes in the parents' lives but in our case I am still bleeding from all the pain he has caused me. I cannot be his friend. I do not feel safe around him and I feel very blessed to have the restraining order in place. As for my son, I do not wish to encourage him to have a relationship with his father, absolutely not. My son needs to heal and open his heart to his father when he is ready. And finally, my last message from me to my husband, please tell him, "Parenting is a privilege and he has lost it for now. Thank you, again, for all your help. God bless you and your children. Have a great day."

My dear God, the look on the faces of both attorneys was unforgettable. All she said was, "God bless you, too." We left and my attorney told me my words were just flawless. He said he was very impressed with how I remained polite, calm, and assertive all while keeping the tone of compassion in my voice. I told him, it was all possible because of my beloved God. He told me i should become a motivational speaker for abused woman. I thanked him, and told him that is in my bucket list. Thank you for this amazing day, dear God. Good night.

The next few weeks were just the same. They were all long days with too much to do and too much to worry about. I had this ongoing anxiety about my husband's criminal case. I was very angry that he had not settled the case by pleading guilty. I just didn't want him to go to jail. It would make my kids very upset -- actually my son did not care but my daughter cared deeply. I just wanted everything to stop. He would be out of my life, out of my sight, and I would get my son's full physical and legal custody. The fact that he was trying to drag everything on was killing me. My attorney's fees were getting out of control and though he deserved to get paid for doing what he was doing, it was just too much for me to afford.

My poor mother was trying so hard to help me during this difficult time but, I kept feeling the same anger and resentment toward her. I could harbor no tolerance for her explanations. In my broken damaged heart, she messed up my life and she was now trying to help me push through the storm that she created. I called my sister and brother few times, begged them to tell my mother to go back home but they simply told me her intentions were to help me through this challenging time. They also reminded me that my son needed her, too. I felt guilty for not wanting to be around her then I realized I did not want to be around anybody. I stopped going to almost all the birthday parties and social gatherings to which I had been invited. I felt out of place in all social gatherings and just wanted to be home by my son and my dog. Here is what I did find helpful: praying, taking long bubble baths, crying, and listening to classical music, worship music, and Madonna. Do not get me wrong, I never regret my decision to get a divorce. I was just angry for staying so long. I hated that I had been so weak for so long. I hated that I had given 21 years of my prime years to someone so heartless. I hated myself for not protecting my children sooner. I resented the fact that my mother had tried so hard to get rid of me when I was 19 years old just because I was beautiful. Was my marriage to this mean man my punishment from God for having a beautiful face? I cried for my son, who is going through the same experiences as I had at exactly the same age he is now. I was angry at myself for being in such denial and only day-dreaming that he would change. I was sad for my pure ignorance. Thank God for my job. I loved, and still do love, my job. My job has been a great escape from my own reality. I am so happy I didn't tell a lot of people about all of this chaos. My loving therapist helped me every week with all of it. It was around this time that I had another really strange dream.

My Dream

My children, husband, and I are on vacation at some nice tropical location close to the ocean. Upon exiting the hotel room, I come across a frightening man dressed in dark draping clothing and a mask appropriate for a Halloween party. Approaching me, he asks permission to join my family for our day at the beach. He reveals that he is lonely and has no one and though his face is hidden behind a terrifying mask, it is clear to me that he is sad. Despite being frightened by everything about him -- everything looked peculiar and nothing seemed right about the situation—I do not have the heart to reject him. The despondency in his hollow eyes and in the tone of his voice is obvious. I grab his hand and insist that he join. Overcome with happiness, he lets go of my hands and jumps into the ocean. When he does, though, the normally blue ocean water becomes darker and turns a shade of navy, then eventually to pure black. Furious that I have ruined the vacation, my husband screams at me, "Who is the loser you have brought?" His yelling makes the children cry. Even our intimidating guest begins to cry, repeating over and over, "I'm so sorry. I'm sorry." Ashamed at my husband's behavior, I beg him not to hurt the feelings of our children or the feelings of the mystery man but my husband refuses to listen. This infuriated me and I lose it. "Stop it!" I cry out, "Stop hurting the people around you! I am not sorry for including this poor person on our family beach day. He is here to stay and if you are not happy about it, you can go to another beach and fuck off!" With that, he becomes quite and busies himself with unpacking our things. Almost immediately, the water color changes back to its beautiful blue color.

The Translation

According to Sue the frightening depressed creature was a dreamed-up manifestation of the part of me that has always felt bad and disgusted with myself. Sue said," It is the broken and damaged part of you that has been lonely and has always strived to do anything your husband wanted to do to earn inclusion. You kept doing, following his orders just to keep him happy. You felt so bad about yourself for letting him treat you like that. You were afraid to see the ugly truth about your spirit and what he had done to you and your dreams. You didn't have the guts to face all the sad realities about your marriage. You kept hiding under a mask. You did not want to let go of the mask even when you were alone. You were ashamed of yourself. When you screamed at your husband, that was your masculine side, the side you are dealing with more often. That is the part that reached out for help, went to the police station, and got your husband out of the house. That is the side you want to get used to. The little broken 19-year-old teen bride is all grown up now and is not taking orders from her abuser anymore. She is a beautiful, smart, educated woman who has a voice not only for her ugly past, but also for her blossoming future."

I cried because she was so right. My Dear God, only you have been my witness to every single moment of my life; you know those dark days filled with weeping, self-disgust, fake smiles, and a loveless marriage. You know about my ongoing struggles to make him notice me and to make him understand I like to be hugged once in a while, I liked to be acknowledged. You know about my on going feeling that I did not want to grow old with him, my wondering where I could possibly go, my fears of all the what-ifs, my daily efforts to do whatever I could to ensure that my kids did not feel my broken heart, my shame for not being able to provide a safe and loving home for my family. Oh, my dear God, you know I could go on and on. You know how hard I prayed you would change me and my life. My dear beloved God, I thank you for all you have done in my life.

3/18/08

IN MY BEDROOM

Dear God, he finally pled guilty and did not push the trial. Thank you. The people at the Victim Assistance Program called and reported that he had pled guilty for disturbing the peace. I thank you, dear God, for ending this phase of my life and protecting my children. The last thing my children and I needed was for this pain to continue. My husband had been planning to move on to a criminal court hearing. His criminal attorney had even called my daughter a few times to ask her to prepare to go to court in order to testify. Dear God, with all the anger I had towards my husband, I hoped he would escape jail-time since that would end up hurting my daughter even more but you handled it in your own way, just as I had prayed.

I still have a hard time calling myself a victim knowing that everything that has happened to me will, in the end and with your divine love, will strengthen me and I am deeply grateful. Victim? No. My story is not about "poor me." It is about "greatly blessed me."

My husband must complete 10 days of community service and another year of anger management class, parenting class, and batterer's treatment. Additionally, he must pay $2400 for my therapy. The best part of the sentence was the extension of his restraining order to three years. Thank you, my beloved God. Finally he has admitted to disturbing my peace!

4/9/2008, 8:55 AM
COURTHOUSE COFFEE SHOP

I am waiting for my attorney to arrive. I do not want to go to the courtroom without him. I need him next to me. Dear God, I just saw my husband and his attorney. My husband looks very sad and I am actually sorry to see him in pain. Dear God please wipe clean all the negative energy between us. I am praying that today he will let go of me and my children. I cannot keep paying my attorney. Please make my husband understand it is done and he needs to move forward. My attorney is walking towards me. We are going into the courtroom. Dear Father, I thank you for this very special moment.

Dear God I am sitting here in the courtroom. I am grateful to you and to all my guardian angels. I feel love, peace, and victory. I am grateful for the bruise he created on my leg with the water bottle. I am grateful to my friend, Karen, who pushed me to go to school. I am happy to be here right now and to see what the law will do to protect me. Dear God, with your help I want to use all that I have learned to help other abused women and children. My attorney and my husband's attorney have walked outside of the courtroom to speak to each other. My husband has gone, too. He is talking very loudly. I can hear him. The court is on break. Oh, my dear God, I can hear him; he is yelling at his attorney that he wants to end everything today. My attorney is back and calls to me to talk. My attorney tells me my husband is very angry and wants to have a hearing today. He wants his son today. Dear God,

The Breakthrough

I am cold and I am shaking. My attorney is sitting next to me and I have asked him to pray for me. He is a pastor at his church and he holds my hand and prays quietly. Dear God, why am I so frightened by my husband? I have changed. I am not the same 19-year-old, hopeless, lost, fatherless little girl with no hope, with no support from my family, lost in my husband's ugly world. I am 41 years old. I have found myself in you. I am not alone. I have my spiritual family right here in the U.S. and my kind and loving family in Iran. I have two amazing kids who look up to me and I am their rock. They need me to do this right the first time. I am going to stay firm and fight with everything I have if I have to and I know you are in charge. My attorney has talked to the other attorney and the judge. It seems that we are going to have a meeting with a mediator soon.

4/13/08

My attorney called me and told me I have to go to court to learn of the court mediator's recommendation regarding custody of my son. Because my husband's criminal case has finished, we can move forward on the divorce and child custody proceedings. I must go, again, to court.

4/24/08, 3:50 PM
MEDIATION OFFICE, ORANGE COUNTY COURTHOUSE

I have just finished talking to the court mediator. I have told her I want full physical custody of my son and she told me that my husband wants 50/50 custody. Because we cannot agree on the terms, my husband will fight for custody. I thank her and tell her I will wait to hear from my attorney.

4/24/08, 10:00 PM
MY BEDROOM

My dear God, it was so sad to see my husband looking as sad as he did. I was given some peace of mind when the court mediator gave me the option to be interviewed separately. I even accepted the offer to be escorted by a police officer from the mediator office to the parking lot. Dear God, it's good but it saddens me at the same time. I have so much fear about what his anger could push him to do to me and the children. I know he is bleeding because he absolutely detests not getting what he wants. I told my therapist that I sometimes fear that he might enter the house through a side window and come for us at gunpoint. She suggested informing the police, praying, installing an alarm system and to not to let the fears get to me. It feels terribly wrong that I need a police officer to protect me against the father of my children. I am praying for peace, understanding, acceptance, and an ending to this marriage. Thank you, my dear God.

5/01/08, 11:30
A CAFE IN NORDSTROM

My attorney told me the hearing is in four days. He asked if I would like to meet to go over all the details or if we should just talk briefly on the phone. I agreed to go over the material on the phone. I feel prepared. I am just worried about my kids. My attorney told me it would be a good idea to have my children with me in court so they could testify against their father. He said if I wanted full physical custody of my son, it would be good to have him there. Right now, I am meeting with my friend, Karen, for lunch. I want to know what she thinks about the idea.

5/3/08, 10:30 PM
MY BEDROOM

Dear God I am feeling anxious. I keep hearing different advice from different people. Karen has told me I should not take my kids to court at all. It will damage them for life. I respect her opinion and I know she is 20 years older than I am and has more life experiences. My attorney called me two days ago to tell me that my husband has lined up 10 people to testify on his behalf: his father, two sisters and their husbands, our neighbor, his cousin, and three parents from my son's soccer team. This worries me and gives me much anxiety. Another friend, Jane, has suggested that I bring my children along. Although my attorney tells me it would be like the icing on the cake, we do not have to do anything if my heart does not feel right. He believes listening to my heart is the answer to all of my questions. Dear God, I am going to pray all day tomorrow. I know you will talk to me. I will call my attorney tomorrow at 6:00 pm to let him know what you want me to do. At the mean time, dear Father, please protect my kids through this entire experience. You know their hearts are broken so I ask you to please help them to put the pieces back together. They need you and I do thank you from the bottom of my heart for this moment of freedom. I am deeply grateful.

5/4/08, 8:35 PM
THE FAMILY ROOM

My dear God, my attorney asked to talk to my son on the phone just to see how my son was feeling about all these issues and my son agreed to do this. They talked for only a few minutes. Then, my son gave me the phone and went back to his homework. He seemed very calm and went on with his normal activities. My attorney told me my son sounded very strong, peaceful, and insightful and he even asked if he could come to court to have a one-on-one meeting with the judge. He is very ready to ask the judge for help. He wants to live with me. To him, his father died a long time ago. My attorney said bringing my son to court would only help. He also told me my daughter does not have to come.

According to him we have a very good, clear case. We have nothing to worry about. All the witnesses my husband is bringing to the court tomorrow are irrelevant. My attorney is convinced tomorrow's judge knows what he is talking about and that all judges are like God in the courtrooms. They are smart, educated, and extremely experienced about what they are doing. He also explained that because domestic violence always occurs indoors and none of my husband's witnesses have ever lived with us for a prolonged period of time, I do not have to worry about any of them. Dear God, I feel good and at peace. I will take my son.

I will call Karen's husband, Jim, to ask him to come with us to the courts. Since the divorce, I asked Jim to spend time with my son at least once a week. I feel that it would be good for my son. Three weeks after my separation from my husband, Karen invited me and the kids to their beautiful beach house. We loved it. The main goal for me was to see how my son would act around Jim. Oh dear God, it was so amazing to see how much fun my son had with Jim. I was so happy that tears of joy streamed down from my cheeks. Jim invited us all to go to the beach in pillow covers. We put our whole bodies in the pillow covers, which was not easy, and then tried to go to the water and let the waves take us around. I tried twice and liked it but became tired and just wanted to enjoy the interactions between Jim and my children. Thank you, Father, for bringing Jim into our lives. For my children, they have lost their father, paternal grandfather, and they never got to meet my father. However, having Jim engage with my kids is just magnificent. Since that August day last year, Jim has been visiting my son at least once a week to go out to eat, play games, talk, and just hang out. The best part is that they share an interest in world history and geography and Jim has proven himself to be the perfect teacher for my son. Jim and Karen travel frequently and upon their return, they always bring back interesting stories and souvenirs for my son to show him that they have not forgotten about him. They could talk for hours about so many things. I love watching them. My son always looks forward to Jim's visits. I am deeply grateful to Jim for doing what he has been doing for my son for the past year. I am also thankful for

Karen for sharing him with my son. Jim was the kind person who called a week before Christmas to discuss bringing his Christmas tree to our house for decorating. I had no idea Christmas was happening so soon and I had no energy to do anything about it. Thanks to Jim, the decorations all came along without having to worry about anything. The tree looked amazing. Dear God, thank you.

5/5/08, 9:00 AM
COURT COFFEE SHOP

Dear God I am sitting in this coffee shop and feeling very anxious. I woke up early this morning to go for a walk and during the walk I began to cry so hard from feelings of weakness. I began to wonder if I could successfully protect my son. I had waited so long to be free from my husband. I ask you to bless me. Dear father I know you have our best interest at heart. After my walk, I came home and took a long bubble bath. Water always helps me wash away my anxiety. I asked my son once more if he was sure he wanted to go to court with me and he said he wanted to defend himself. Dear God I hope I did the right thing by bringing him. Now we are here. I am so grateful that Jim is sitting at a table next to me and playing Risk with my son. My son looks peaceful. Thank you, Father. My attorney is going to come here to take me inside the court room.

9:47 AM

My attorney, Sam, informed me that the 18 other cases before mine would force me to wait a long time and I would even need to return. Dear God, I leave it to you. This is your battle, not mine. I am feeling better as I am listening to Pachelbel's Canon. Some might say this is an inappropriate song to listen to with it being used so commonly for weddings. However, for me, this is the best possible song I could possibly listen to at this very moment. You know, my Father, how bad I wanted this day to come. This song is making my heart to sing again. It speaks to me about the many blessed and joyful memories

I have waiting for me. It allows me to imagine a life without fear. I ask you to bless my son with love, protection, and guidance as he testifies. I imagine he will be using all of his natural gifts from you on this very special day. I imagine he will combine all his magnificent gifts from you to get him through this and I pray that he becomes a compassionate husband, father, and leader. I have big hopes and dreams for him and he has big dreams for himself, too. He strives to study at the nation's top universities. I thank you for putting these big dreams into his courageous heart. I know with your blessings and his desire to do great things, he will be become someone even more magnificent.

I am still listening to Canon, which makes me think about my sweet, dedicated, hard-working, responsible daughter. She is not here today. Sam said she would not need to come. I am imagining all the pain she had to go through since she was only two years old, seeing how her father made me cry and frightened all the time. I feel guilty for not protecting her. As a mother, I feel that I was put here to do whatever I can to protect my babies against any pain but I was too weak to keep her away from the constant anger, criticism, and name-calling from her father. Yet, she knows I have always loved her more than I do my own life. This is something both of my children have known since they began calling me "mom." Today, though, while I am listening to this joyous song, part of me is very angry at myself for staying too long in such a toxic environment. Part of me is still worried about my lovely daughter and her future but I cannot linger on negativity. I am going to use this very special moment to enjoy my music and let my imagination roam wild. I imagine my daughter graduating from university next year. I see her using her tender, loving heart to do something extraordinary for this world. I see her changing people's lives in positive directions with all that she has learned and your blessings. She will combine all these and become an ideal role model for young adults. I know she is blessed with great discipline and a heart of gold. Dear father she is going to have an interview next week for an amazing internship opportunity in Washington D.C. I am just so grateful for her. Dear God, I imagine her being proud of herself everyday. I remember when she got accepted to her university and his family nearly nagged her to become a doctor. She tried. She studied biology for two years but it just did not seem to fit her. She went as far as interning at some local hospitals, too. She came to me and revealed to me that she did not have a taste for all of her biology and chemistry classes but had already begun taking other classes in political science, which she enjoyed. I told her she might want to think about changing her major to something she had a fire for. She cried. She had been carrying all of this stress and anxiety regarding how her father might react. And he did find out. The day before I got the restraining order, he went online to look for her grades and her academic progress. He completely lost it. He started calling her names and putting her down. He told her she has no right to change her major from Biology to Political Science. He was yelling for hours and demanded that she return everything back to what it had been. Then, he insulted her with comparisons to "her loser mother" and said she would never get anywhere in life. Dear Father, this beautiful song is helping me to imagine nothing but peaceful days ahead of her. I know you have amazing plans in store for her. Dear God I imagine the day my children marry gentle and loving people. I pray their marriages are nothing like mine. Dear God, I thank you. Sam is coming to take me inside the court.

2:45 PM
COURTROOM

Oh, dear God, I am sitting inside the court room. A lot has happened since this morning. At 11:30 am, I testified and it was very difficult at first as everyone in my husband's family was sitting directly in front of me. He looked angry and his attorney had a hard time restraining him. Sam asked me basic questions and I answered with short sentences and a calm voice. I kept reminding myself that you, my Father, were in charge. I remembered Madonna in an interview stating that from all difficult situations, something positive always results. Thank you, my Father, for this very moment that I am trying to get this man out of my life for good.

It is close to lunch time so we finish up a little early. Sam approached me to inform me of my husband's attorney's wish to speak with my son. My son refused the request and I refused to force him to do anything he had no wish to do. Thus, Sam left us for a while, went back to the courtroom, talked to the judge, and expressed what he thought we should do, which was to let my son decide how he wanted to express his opinions about his father. It took a long time and the judge wanted to talk to my son personally. My husband's attorney did not like this idea, though Sam did. The judge agreed to have the two attorneys talk to my son in the court coffee shop. He emphasized that my attorney would be in charge and made sure Sam knew to stop as soon as my son wished to stop. Whether or not I was present for all this would be up to me but my husband was not allowed to take part in it.

My son was having fun playing with Jim -- God bless Jim for keeping him busy. I asked my son if he wanted me to be there. He said he felt comfortable with Sam and said I would not need to be there. While they interviewed my son for about 10 minutes, I just sat with Jim. As soon as they finished, my husband's attorney came to me and told me, "Congratulations. Your son is truly one of a kind." I thanked her. I told her, "I feel very blessed to be his mother, and it is God who makes my son very unique. God bless your children, too. You seem like a very strong, hard working mother." She looked at me, was quiet, and thanked me for my kindness. About 30 minutes after all this, while I was sitting with Jim and my son, waiting for our turn to go back inside the courtroom, Sam pulled me aside and told me my husband's attorney wanted the four of us to talk to see if we could arrive at a resolution. For just a few moments, I was frightened at the thought of sitting face-to-face with my husband. Then, I asked Sam to pray for peace and courage in me. He did, and then told me how brilliant my son had done in the meeting with the two attorneys and that I had done a fine job raising him. A few minutes later, I found myself sitting face-to-face with my husband. He looked broken. He had lost some weight and as I started to feel sorry for him, he opened his mouth and out came his condescending tone of voice and I went back to August

6th, 2007, the day I went to the police station. My compassion left and I felt pain, anger, and rage. I was ready to just get up and say, "get out of my face." but I did not. I just took a deep breath, practiced deep breathing exercises, and got focused on you, oh dear God. I prayed for you to bless me with peace, courage, and strength and you did. Thank you. When he opened his mouth, only nonsense spewed out. However, because of you, my Lord, I remained quiet for 23 minutes and let him talk. He said, "I want joint physical and legal custody. I want all the rugs, fifty percent of the furniture, two cars and if you do not agree to my terms, I will not give you half of the house. I have documents that prove I bought that house with my own money before I met you. So, do not push your luck, and agree with everything I am saying."

I took a deep breath and asked you for help and this was my answer, "I did listen to everything you said for at least 20 minutes and I am asking for you to give me just four minutes of your undivided attention -- and I will start timing myself. First of all, I am not your naive, hopeless, weak 19-year-old teenaged wife anymore. I am 41 years old, and I am not broken anymore. I have God with me and I know I am part of Him. Having said that, half of the house is mine; I earned that. Stop trying to frighten me with your nonsense. This is not a charity event. I earned half of everything and I will get that. As far as the rugs, furniture, and the cars go, all I can say is, "Wow." And for joint physical and legal custody of our son, absolutely not. Parenting is a privilege and you lost it. I will fight with absolutely everything I have to keep you away from him because my hope for him is that he will be nothing like you."

Then I looked at my watch and told Sam, "I am done. It took about four and a half minutes for that whole thing." As Sam and I left the table, Sam looked at me and told me, "You did just great," then returned to court.

I am now just waiting to see what is going to happen. Sam told me we are going to go inside in about 10 minutes. Dear God, thank you.

4:35 PM

I just took the stand again. It was time for my husband's attorney to cross-examine me. It was very easy. She began by asking me why I had waited 20 years to get the divorce. If he was such a bad husband, why did I apply for the restraining order and the divorce only upon getting my job? She accused me of lying, that I had actually planned all of this for other reasons. According to her, my husband was accusing me of wanting full physical custody of my son so I would be able to take him to Iran, or to another state, and cut all ties between him and his father.

Before I could say anything, the judge addressed the issue, "Ms. Hashem, as you know, the most common reason women stay in violent relationships is the lack of financial stability. Having said that, this case sounds very common." The attorney responded, "Well, Your Honor, Ms. Zahra works in the field of counseling. She has volunteered in domestic violence shelters. Why, as an expert in the field, has she waited so long?" The judge looked at me for an answer. I took a deep breath, reminded myself that God was in control of everything, and said, "I did an internship at a shelter for abused women and children in 2003. At the time, I was a full-time student with no job, no financial stability, and no support from family. I was frightened to make any move but I knew I would be able to get myself out of this mess once I finished my education and found a stable job so that I could take care of my son." The judge looked at me and said to Ms. Hashem, "Exactly what I said to you, Ms. Hashem. Just to make sure everybody is clear on this, what Ms. Zahra did is a great example of a woman in a domestic violence relationship."

Ms. Hashem revealed some love letters and cards I had given to my husband a long time ago. She pointed out that my marriage must have been a loving union. Otherwise, I would not have written those love letters to my husband. I responded, "You cannot blame me for keeping hope that he would learn to control his anger and change."

The judge looked at the dates on the cards and asked, "Ms.Hashem do you have any new evidence from the last two to five years?" She didn't. I remained calm. Then, it was my brother-in-law's turn to testify -- this was the calm, self-contained, Caucasian brother-in-law. He said he was in shock to hear about the divorce. He stated , my husband could not possibly hurt anyone and the restraining order made no sense to him. He was convinced that my husband loved his son and, thus, deserved to have half custody of him.

After my brother-in-law finished his statements, it was time for my poor 80-year-old father-in-law to testify. As expected, he only spoke of great things about his son. I do not blame him. He denied and lied about ever having witnessed any violence towards my children and me. I just lost it. I calmed myself and asked Sam to ask him about a phone call from me in August of 2006 at 6:30am in the morning. "Was that normal for your daughter-in-law to call you that early just for a hello?"

Oh, my dear God, my poor father-in-law's face changed to a look of fright. I hated my husband for doing this to him. He said it was nothing, that he came to the house because they were having car problems and my husband wanted to use his car. My father-in-law was lying so badly. His face was revealing more than his words were. Sam asked him calmly to tell the truth and my father-in-law said it was just some misunderstanding about cars and that was it. On a slip of paper I passed to Sam I had written that I wanted to take the stand to speak on the issue.

It was very common for my husband to take the car keys anytime he was in a mood, which was very often in the last five years. Last year, it was a Monday morning and I had to drive my daughter to the train station by 7:00 am, come home to get my son ready for summer camp, drop him off at 7:45 am, then drive to work which was about 30 minutes away. So, when he demanded the car keys at 6:15, I just looked at him and said, "Please. Today is Monday and I have to drive the kids to where they need to be then drive myself to work. I cannot be late." He said, "Fuck you," and ordered me to take off my clothes.

He had done this so many times but I did not know there was a word for such an event. Later, during my internship at the domestic violence center, I learned the word for what he was doing, forcing me to have sex with him against my will. I would learn, later, the word for it, "rape." It wasn't until I was in my 30s that I learned that I had a right to deny sex.

"Please, I am going to be late," I begged him to let me go and asked for the car keys. He attacked me and, without going into unnecessary details, he raped me. It was 6:30am and he told me he would not give me the car keys. He said I needed to learn to use public transportation like other people. That was when I decided to call his father, who arrived in about 15 minutes. The first words out of his mouth were, "Why do you bother your husband?" Then he went to talk to his son.

With the car keys in hand, my husband demanded that I apologize and say, "I eat your shit," all in front of my father-in-law. I wept tears which flowed like a waterfall.

I said to the judge, "I needed the car keys to take care of my kids and go to work. So I said to my husband, after he had just raped me 30 minutes prior -- and I was still hating my body for being touched by him -- and in front of his father, "I am sorry and I eat your shit." I could not control myself in the courtroom. My weeping must have affected the people in the room for when I looked up, they all looked uncomfortable. "Your Honor," I said, "My tears are tears from joy. I am very happy to be here right now in front of you, and making my voice heard." The judge looked uncomfortable and said we would continue the next day.

I am sitting in the courtroom waiting for Sam to finish his talk with Ms. Hashem. I am tired but feel relieved. I thank you, my beloved Father, for holding my hands through the storm. I felt your presence for the entire time. This is your battle, not mine. I cannot wait to go get my son from Jim and Karen's house, take him home, and let go of all the things that happened today.

5/6/08, 11:30 AM
STARBUCKS

My dear Father, I am getting ready for another day. I met with Sam this morning at 8:30am at his office to prepare for today. I told him about the six tapes of private phone conversations my husband had recorded. He had recorded my phone calls with my family and friends from April through July in 2007. Sam informed me it is against the law to record anyone's voice without his or her permission. He said that we did not need to bring them up in court for two reasons: first we had a clean and clear case of domestic violence. The judge, and everyone else, was touched by my testimony so we were in a great place and we would get what we want. Secondly, he could face jail-time for his crime and that is not what I wanted as it would have long-term effects on my children. Sam instructed me to bring the tapes in case we absolutely needed them.

Sam also spoke with my daughter and it was his opinion that she was not ready to testify against her father. However, she didn't need to be there because we had been doing just fine. We would only use her if we became desperate.

I was anxious and worried. I confided to Sam that I was feeling lonely. After all, he had his entire family there for him; I was there alone. Sam looked at me and said to me, "You are the strongest client I have ever had in my 15 years of practicing law. Do not worry. He could have 100 people next to him but he will still look weak, frightened, and guilty. The judge could see that very clearly yesterday. You have God, your guardian angels, your true story of 21 years of ongoing pain, and you have me. We are going to be just fine. This is your chance to share your pain with the judge." He added, "I see you giving workshops all over the world helping abused women and children. God will use this to make you stronger and He will use you to help many more people. Just hang in there." I thanked him for being there with me today and I thanked him for believing me, and then I asked him to pray.

I am feeling very good about all this. I got a call from my lovely soul-sister, Tania. She is very kind, caring, and spiritual. We met at the hair salon where I had worked for a long time and we connected immediately and bonded over our love for you, Lord. I had opened up to her a few times when I was very sad about my marriage. She always prayed for me and reminded me that God would show me the way on His own time. I feel like we have known each other for a very long time.

I was up again early this morning praying and, all of a sudden, I received a call from her. She had called because she had had a feeling I needed some sisterly love. Oh my Father, that was so kind of her. I loved talking to her. She said she would pray for me all day. I received a few more phone calls from my sister, brother, mother, and some great friends here. I thank you, Father, for all their love and support. I am feeling better now. I will be going to court after 2:00 pm. I pray for peace today.

2:20 PM
COURTROOM L71

Dear Father, I am sitting in the courtroom next to Sam. I will be taking the stand in about 10 minutes. Sam prepared me for the cross-examination by Ms. Hashem. My in-laws are all here, except for a few, and they all are looking at me with such hatred and anger. I am sorry for all the pain I have caused my husband's family. I wish they would be more understanding about all of this. I just cannot continue to prostitute myself. My spirit cannot take it anymore. I am a mother and I need to try to do my best to provide and promote a safe and loving environment for my children and I hope they forgive me for waiting too long to do this. I pray that Judge Smith connects with me and sympathizes with me. Dear Father, I ask that you open up his heart to the truth and let him be guided only by you. I made a promise to my son when he was 10 years old and we were hiding from my husband in his room. I had promised him that as soon as I finished school and found a job to support us, if his father could not change, I would divorce him and fight for full custody. Dear Father, please help me to keep my promise to him.

7:00 PM
HOME

Oh, my Dear Father, I am so happy to be home. What a long day it was today. Ms. Hashem did such a lousy job today that part of me thinks deep down in her heart, she wants me to get everything I want. I think she is on my side. I would hate to feel that she is taking on my husband's narrow-minded point-of-view. Today, she asked me the most nonsensical and irrelevant questions. The judge yelled at her few times, but she kept making the judge angry. Finally, the the judge called her and Sam to his side and they talked for a while. It was hard for me to sit in front of all my enemies. They were all staring at me. I am sorry, Lord, for calling them my enemies and I pray that you help them to forgive me and accept me as I am.

Ms. Hashem's questioning today was the same as it was yesterday -- I mean exactly the same. She said it seemed I had planned this divorce long time ago. She asked why, as a professional counselor, I did not approach the police long ago. I just looked at her and gave her very brief answers with an assertive voice. I just told her I was not ready. I explained that I filed for a restraining order seven weeks after I got my full-time job, which provided me with medical benefits.

While she was insinuating that I had planned this divorce, in my head, I was saying, "Of course I did. I started praying that God would change my husband almost 19 years ago, but when I realized he would not change, in 2000 my prayers changed. I was asking God to show me a way out of this marriage I was in."

I prayed, oh Lord, to get this man out of my sight and out of my life. I was so lost and sad. You pushed me to go to school and my education became my light at the end of the tunnel. I kept pushing myself for seven years. I began with baby steps and widened each subsequent step, thank you, my Father, for finding a safe escape from the sad married life I was in. I did not want to get tied up in affairs, drugs, or alcohol as a way to escape this man. I wanted to be sober and clear-minded every step of the way. Though there was much pain for me to endure, you provided me with my amazing children and educational opportunities to encourage me.

After my testimony, the court therapist took the stand to share her opinion about her interview with my son, husband, and me. I prayed that she would collaborate my story, share with everyone my son's pain, and reveal my husband's lies. I was told that her testimony would be very important to the case. During her talk, I was too anxious to listen. I only wanted to zone out and pray, and I did. She was there for a while and though I was very close to her I just could not hear her. I was asking you, my Father, to guide all her words, and to use her to make the judge see more truth in my story.

My husband looked so angry that I thought he might hit his attorney. The judge ordered Ms. Hashem to restrain her client or to take him outside. Sam looked at me and said that we got what we wanted. While Sam and I walked out, I asked him to tell me what the court therapist said. Surprised that to hear that I had not been paying attention, he told me that she related the entire truth to everyone in that courtroom. He said she made it very clear that, in her years of experience working with domestic violence cases, she believed this to be the classic case. My son had told her he does not feel safe around his father, and his father had physically, verbally, and emotionally abused him, his sister, and his mother. She had told everyone that she believed my son should live with me full time. She thought it best that I have the full physical and legal custody of my son. Any visitation with the father should be monitored by professionals and limited, at least in the beginning, to one hour a week. Oh, my Father, thank you. This is exactly what I had prayed for.

5/7/08, 2:45 PM
COURTROOM

Dear Father, this is going to be the last day of the trial. These last two days have been filled with your favor and I thank you. I am sitting next to Sam who is preparing to cross-examine my husband. It is so sad to see how hard my husband tries to lie. He is not ready to be healed. Sam is asking him very basic questions and he looks so lost trying to fight with the truth. He says he has always loved me and our kids and he believes that what I did, filing for a restraining order and divorce, was all the result of my own stress with graduate school and work. Well, maybe he always loved me and my kids in his own sick way. He denies any history of rape and domestic violence. The judge is looking very frustrated. Sam is asking him about his work history and why he has not worked these last few years. Sam is trying to get onto the issue of child support. When Sam asks him if he is planning to pay any child support, my husband answers, "She works full time as a therapist. Why doesn't she use her hair dressing skills and work weekends, too, as a hair dresser?" This is when Sam lost it -- it was the first time I had seen him lose his calmness -- and said, "Your Honor, my client works 40 hours a week and is going to take care of her son full-time. How could he have the audacity to imply that my client needs to work on weekends, too?" The judge agrees with Sam. At this point my husband is just sitting there in his own denial. His attorney looks very uncomfortable. His family members look sad. The judge states that she wants to go back to the domestic violence issues. Sam asks my husband what happened on August 3rd, 2007. My husband does not seem to understand that the more he talks of his nonsense, the more he frustrates the judge. Dear Father, I cannot write. I am feeling very dizzy.

3:45 PM
COURT ROOM

Dear Father, it is just hurting to see that he is still not ready to take responsibility of his actions. Sam tried to help him to open up and tell the truth, but my husband is running away from truth as fast as he can. I do not know where his destination is. He has lost his wife, children, and what is left? Maybe he just does not know how to bond with people or even his loved ones. I just reminded myself of that poor young girl that he left behind in England while she was carrying his baby boy. He married me and never tried to even meet his baby, who was an exact copy of him. Yes, he is a man with no heart, no values, no ethics, nothing. Dear Father, please keep him far from me and my kids. Please take him far away and keep him happy, but very far form all of us. Dear Father, I am sitting in front of the court of law to fight, not only for my children and myself, but also the young pregnant girl and for my children's half-brother, who is now probably 22 years old. I am also going to sit here and remember all my sisters who have been raped, abused, insulted by men like my husband. Dear Father, I am going to use all this pain to grow and try to be a source of hope to all the abused women and children in the world. Dear Father, you have big goals for me in life.

Sam is going back to August 3rd, 2007 again. This time he is not stopping. The judge asks to review the police report from that day and the pictures of my leg. She instructs Sam to continue and he does not waste any time. Sam asks my husband why he pled guilty for disturbing the peace in a criminal court two months ago if nothing happened that night. "Why did you agree to do 10 days of community service picking up trash in the parks and streets. Why are you taking anger management classes, parenting classes, and batterer's treatment if all you did was throw a water bottle at your wife? If that's all you did, then you are paying a huge price for that," he says. This is amazing the way Sam is trying to show the judge my husband's real character. The judge is still looking at the reports while listening to everything. Now she asks to see the copy of the criminal court records and my husband's written report of that day. Father, I thank you for everything.

4:24 PM
COURT ROOM

Dear Father, we are waiting for the judge. She is reading and writing something. Sam is sitting next to me. I have asked him to pray for me again which he does. Dear Father, please keep my husband far from me and my kids.

4:37 PM
COURT ROOM

Thank you, my Father. I am so happy. I have received full physical custody. Dear Lord, thank you for letting the judge see the truth. Thank you for keeping this man out of my life and my children's lives. We are running out of time. The court will be closed soon. The judge stated my son's visitations with his father will be monitored and my husband does not like this. We are instructed to return on May 13th, 2008 to end this whole thing. Sam tells me the physical custody issue is more that one hundred percent done. I got it. I cannot wait to tell my son. I am so hungry. I have not been able to eat for three days. I called Jane and told her the good news. She invited me and my son to her home for dinner. Dear Father, thank you. I need to make a lot of phone calls and thank a lot of wonderful people for their prayers.

5/10/08, 10:30 PM
MY BEDROOM

Dear Father, I feel at peace. I thank you for the success in obtaining full custody of my precious son. My Lord, I know you will provide the strength and courage for me to do what I have to do everyday. I am hoping to be a loving, strong, and compassionate single mother. I lost my father when I was eleven years old and, by coincidence, my son is the same age. Dear Father, I know his heart is broken; help me to make his broken heart heal one day at a time. Help me to help him to erase one bad memory at a time and replace all the bad memories with more joyful, peaceful memories. I have taken him back to his therapist, against his will. I just wanted to make sure he is fine. The therapist told me not to waste my money or time. "Your son is very happy, content and relaxed. He has no room in his heart for his father. When kids get hit by crises at a young age, they are forced to grow up. If they do not get the love and support from at least one parent on daily basis, they start showing symptoms of depression. Your son has none of these symptoms. He has so many big goals, loves school, and nothing has changed in his daily routine. So, respect his opinion about not needing my help. Your son loves you, and believes you are going to take good care of him." I cried; I was so happy that my son had not been damaged. Dear Father, I will do my best to make his little heart filled with my love.

Many of my married friends are telling me that I should start dating, perhaps find a nice rich man. I just look at them and when they just keep talking nonsense, I just tell them for the next seven years I need to give all my love and attention to my kids, specially my son. He needs me and I need to stay focused during this journey. With your blessing, dear Lord, I am going to make sure to do my best everyday to be there for my kids. I want them to have strong self esteem, love for themselves, big goals, and drive. Thank you, my Father. I have no fears from any other court hearings. I got what I wanted. When I first met Sam, I told him that all I wanted was to keep my husband out of my life for good and to get full physical custody of my son. I got both of those. Thank you, my beloved Father.

5/13/08, 9:00 AM
COURT COFFEE SHOP

Dear Lord, I am waiting for Sam. I thank you for peace. Sam has gone to the court room to see if he and Ms. Hashem can agree on few things. I just saw one of my sisters-in-law walk in to support her brother. I used to be very close to her. She is very peaceful and I used to think she would never harm anyone. She saw me and completely ignored me like she had been doing lately. Sam is walking towards me.

10:30 AM
COURT ROOM

Oh, my Father, nothing is accomplished. My husband is angry as he sits next to his two sisters. His attorney has requested my father-in-law to be the person to monitor my son's visitations with his father. The judge, thankfully, has denied this request. Based on what has been said in the testimonies, the judge sees the father-in-law as weak and unreliable. The judge suggests the idea of monitored visitation at a local counseling office, where a therapist can monitor the father-son interactions. My husband will not like this, though I am fine with the arrangement. We will be back in July to end all this. It feels good to be away from the court for a while.

12/27/2008. BIG ISLAND OF HAWAII

Dear father I am here on this beautiful beach in Hawaii on vacation with my two children. It is raining, and I love it. We just came out of the water. The combination of a bright blue sky, crystal blue water, and the colorful rainbow is just magnificent. I had a dream a while ago that I would be swimming in the rain in the ocean with my kids, without fearing anybody. Thank you my beloved father for letting us be here. Thank you for making my dreams come true one by one in your own timing. It is such a great feeling to be free. Although I was already in the ocean swimming with my kids, the sensation the raindrops gave me was different; it energized my soul and made feel awakened to your amazing miracles. In this moment I came to realize more than ever that I am part of something magnificent! Thank you father.

8/4/12. 6:32 PM MY BACKYARD

Dear father, I thank you for today. I thank you for the amazing road the last 5 years. You have been so good to me. In my wildest dreams I never could have imagined how much you could bless me. Thank you for showing me that the sun will come out after bad, heavy rain.

Thank you for planting the seed of faith in my broken heart. I think about all the reasons why not me? You know after that phone call about my father's death, I was wondering why you did this to me? What did I do wrong to lose such a kind caring father? Why did I have to witness my mother's severe depression since I was only 11? Why did I have to be my beautiful sister's shoulder to cry on since I was 13 years old? Why did I have to see her tears after each time that she got hit by her husband for different reasons? Why I couldn't sleep at night time when I would hear my sweet eight year old brother crying in his sleep and begging my father to come back because he was worry about forgetting his voice? Why did I get married to a man who was 10 years older than me, whom I only knew for weeks? Why did I lose my self respect, my identity, my roots, my spirit, my dreams, hopes and goals to this man? Why did it take from 19 to 40 to finally get it? Why? Why? Why?

Well It took me a long time, but I finally got it. My dear beloved father I know why. I got broken at the age of 11. Since then you have been working in me. I thank you for teaching about pain, sadness, crises, and physical, emotional, sexual, and financial abuse. I thank you for putting me through all this. All these helped me to go after a job, or a mission to help people with broken hearts

Today I am sitting in this beautiful back yard. I am grateful and speechless for all your love in my life. The divorce was finalized on 10/09. I got my son's full physical custody. He is away this weekend to a leadership camp in Northern California. It was by invitation only. With the help of you my dear father he is just doing fantastic. He will be starting 11th grade, loves school, has big dreams, and with your divine blessings, and protection he will be an honorable man. I am so proud to be his mom every single time I see his handsome face. I still call him my brilliant son.

My beautiful angel, my daughter received her bachelor's degree from a great university, followed her heart, and changed her major from something that she was forced to do to something she loved. She followed her passion and is working in Washington, DC. She is also waiting to hear from law schools. She wants to become a policymaker. Thank you, my dear God. She is becoming a very strong, confident, independent young lady. Some times when I look at her big beautiful eyes, I just cannot forget what the doctor told me when she was 2 weeks old, how she had her heart problems, had her open heart surgery before she was 3 years old. Today her heart is going very strong. Thank you father.

I thank you dear God for making my own dreams come true in your own timing. I have no regrets about my past. I am too busy being grateful for now. That phone call made me learn what pain is and how to relate to broken hearts. I work full time as a therapist. The best part of my job is when I know I did my best to be there for my clients. That phone call helped me to be able to talk to my clients on the phone when they are in their crises.

I wake up every day, and I pray that my dear God you use me to help others.

Although I got separated five years ago, and have been divorced since 2009, I am not dating. I am still trying to get to know myself. When my friends and family tell me this is my prime time, I should be searching, fishing, hoping for a suitable boyfriend, or husband, I just look at them and say, "not now". They keep telling me why not now? My answer is, "Well there are a few different reasons. To begin with I am full-time mother, with a very gifted teenage son. I feel like parenting is a privilege and it is a mission. I am grateful to God to be my son's mother. I believe God is using me to shape and nurture this amazing young man. I know my dear God is going to use my son to serve, and help people. This is my homework, and blessing from God to provide, protect, and promote for this special tall handsome young man. What I love the most is his fire to want to learn and the way his eyes sparkle when he learns or hears something new. When he was in kindergarten his teacher said to him, I just want to kiss your beautiful brain. Dear God you have blessed him with amazing talents. Thank you. I want to be the rock he needs to lean on. He lost his father the exact age that I lost my father. Dear God, I want his children to feel loved by him and feel safe next to him. I want him to learn to respect his wife, and all females all the time. I want to make sure he knows what compassion is.

In the past 25 years I feel I have grown to love God more and more. Today I know God is love. I prayed and God replaced all my hate and anger with love and forgiveness towards the people I used to blame for my unhappiness. I know God put them all in my life for his plans. I know he is the director of my life. Today I am grateful to my ex-husband for giving me two amazing kids. I am thankful for the way he pushed me to go to cosmetology school. The way he kept telling me I am uneducated and how he was ashamed to introduce me as his wife, since as a hair dresser I was just washing people's heads and would bring germs home, according to him. I thank him every day for his negative, harsh criticisms. I used to pray that he would die every day. Today I am asking for forgiveness from my dear God. Today in my prayers many times, I am asking my ex-husband to forgive me for any pain I have created for him and his family. I pray God brings peace, joy, and love to his heart.

Today I pray for healing. Today I feel complete. My heart is filled with my beloved father's love. Today I love my mother more than my life. I admire how she sacrificed all her life after my father's sudden death to take care of me and my siblings, although she needed someone to take care of her, and her broken heart. She did her best under the circumstances she was in to give me the best she could afford. Today I feel her broken heart as I walk in her shoes every day. Being a single parent is one of the most rewarding and difficult jobs in the world. My mother had three kids to raise all by herself. She is my hero. She had many many chances to remarry after my father's sudden death, but she told us, she cannot bring another man to our lives until we all are grownups. She told us the last thing she wanted to do was marry someone, and that someone could end up sexually or physically abuse us. She gave us everything she could. Today she feels guilty about my divorce and my sister's divorce. As you remember I used to blame her and I even stopped talking to her when she came to be with me during my divorce. I cried in my room for hours, and kept asking God to replace my anger and hate for my mother with love and forgiveness. It took a while. I needed time, and finally I arrived to have unconditional love and respect for my mother. I admire her big, loving heart. Today when I feel burned out of my daily struggles as a single mom, I call her and she keeps encouraging me.

Today I take full responsibility for the life I am living. Today I am grateful for my weaknesses and my strengths. I love knowing my dear God has blessed me with a job that I can connect with human beings that need to be heard. Today I wake up energized about my day, my life and how I my dear God will continue to bless me.

The reason I am writing this book is to connect and share my journey from darkness to light. I want this book to be used as a helping tool to anyone that has been through severe pain. I want to let my readers know when there is nobody there to listen to you, feel you, and bring comfort to you, all you need is God. All the answers are in this word GOD. Just call him, try to build a relationship with him. Try to be honest and vulnerable. In the dark night and long days all you need is him.

Since I was 21 years old and married with a beautiful baby girl, I knew in my heart I do not want to grow old with my ex-husband. I was desperately thinking about the concept of SOUL MATE. I loved all the romantic movies with the great endings of finding the true romantic love. I knew what I had in my marriage was anything than romantic, so I started day dreaming about all the possibilities of romantic love. I use to cry, happy tears at almost all wedding ceremonies. I still have some happy tears when I see a happy bride and groom, and I pray in my heart for everlasting happiness for them. What is different now in my own heart , is that I do not feel empty anymore. In the last 5 years, since I have been separated from my ex-husband, I have been getting very close and personal with my beloved father. My heart is not broken and it not bleeding. My heart is healed, and is filled with GOD's love.

A few weeks ago while I was journaling, (yes I still journal, thanks to my dear Oprah) I just let go of my pen, and started to have my usual intimate conversations with God. I was so happy, when I came to the conclusion that I may never get married again, because my heart fully belongs to God now. Since my son will be finishing his high school in 2 years, I am thinking about what I would do with my life after he is gone, and all the free time that I would have. While I was writing to God in my journal I started to think about how wonderful it would be if I could join the Peace Corps to help people that need God's love more than anything. This is such a big shift in my life, giving up romantic love for good, and knowing that I am not desperate anymore. My cup is full. In the next two years I would like to open a non-profit organization for abused woman, children and men. I want to help them to transform their lives from inside to outside.

God willing I can use his love to get in to all the broken hearts, and help them to be connected to the source of LOVE. Then I would use my counseling skills to help them forgive, forget and move forward. I also could use my hairdressing skills to transform their outside too. Provide group therapy, career counseling, and unconditional love to help them get to know their own world of possibilities when they know God.

Today I am not angry for losing my father, because his spirit is always with me. I feel blessed to have him in my life for 11 years. He left planet earth at 42 but his legacy is still here. His legacy was to be kind to each other. He used to say we all are God's children, we all are connected, by his love. His best advice to me when I was eight years old was, "God has blessed you with a voice, make sure you never use this voice to hurt anybody, because if you say bad things about God's children this would be an insult to him. So when you open your mouth if you have something nice to say go for it, if you do not, please be quiet." I loved and respected my father so much that I promised him I would do that for him, although I was too young to get the whole meaning behind this. Today as a 45 years old woman, I try to make sure to use my voice, with kind words. I am a work in progress like all of God's children, but I know I'm home.

Acknowledgments

I'd like to thank all my family and friends who have been part of this journey. After reading this book, you do not need to worry about me anymore. As you see, I am home.

I'd like to thank Mrs. Marti Kresse and Ms. Jennifer Park for helping me to edit this book.

I'd like to thank my attorney, Mr. Steven DeWitt, for his hard work throughout my divorce.

I'd like to endlessly thank my children for giving me a reason to get up every day and go through life knowing I'm their mother.